LEITHS

HOW TO COOK
PASTRY

JENNY STRINGER CLAIRE MACDONALD
CAMILLA SCHNEIDEMAN

Photography by Peter Cassidy

Quadrille
PUBLISHING

CONTENTS

NOTES

✻ All spoon measures are level unless otherwise stated:
1 tsp = 5ml spoon; 1 tbsp = 15ml spoon.

✻ Use medium eggs unless otherwise suggested. Anyone who is pregnant or in a vulnerable health group should avoid recipes that use raw egg whites or lightly cooked eggs.

✻ Use fresh herbs unless otherwise suggested.

✻ If using the zest of citrus fruit, buy unwaxed fruit.

✻ Timings are guidelines for conventional ovens. If you are using a fan-assisted oven, set your oven temperature approximately 15°C (1 Gas mark) lower. Use an oven thermometer to check the temperature.

INTRODUCTION

Pastry making is the ultimate culinary alchemy. The same ingredients – flour, fat, salt and liquid – are combined to produce very different results depending on the proportions and varied techniques used. Short crumbly pastries, flaky layered pastries, crisp pastry shells and pie crusts to soak up a delicious filling are all easy to make when you understand the reason for each step and then practise the skills. This book sets out the methods we have tried and tested in our school, where we teach would-be chefs and home cooks the pleasure of making pastries of all different kinds.

Many students start a course at Leiths under the impression that good pastry chefs are born not made, that it is impossible for them to make good pastry. This is just not true. We enjoy teaching our students the basic techniques and see them gain confidence as they practise and master the subject before going on to experiment and create new recipes of their own.

PASTRY QUANTITIES

In this book, recipes refer to a quantity (or a half quantity) of a specific pastry recipe. It is not always practical to make the exact amount needed for a dish, but pastry freezes very well, so if you're using a smaller flan ring, or only need half the quantity of pastry, wrap the rest in cling film and freeze for up to a month. Freeze trimmings too – these often come in handy for decoration, or to patch up any cracks or holes in a pastry case.

Most pastries are made using a rough ratio of half fat to flour, though the enriched pastries have a higher ratio of butter, which gives a richer, shorter crust.

USING BOUGHT PASTRY

Obviously the object of this book is to teach and encourage you to make your own pastries. However, as long as you buy good quality (all-butter) pastry, the results will still be delicious. Some of the recipes call for pastry to be rolled to a specific thickness, particularly puff, so if you are using a ready-rolled pastry, check to see if it requires further rolling before use.

If buying puff pastry in blocks rather than ready-rolled sheets, it is a good idea to cut it into portions before using, depending on what you intend to do with it. As a rough guide, a 500g block of puff pastry can be used to top two family-sized pies, so it makes sense to cut it in half. Wrap one half closely in cling film and freeze for future use.

If using bought filo pastry for a recipe, try to buy the amount you intend to use, or the smallest pack you can for the quantity you need. Although it does freeze if well wrapped in cling film, it still tends to dry out and become brittle.

The core ingredients

FAT

Butter is used in pastries for the delicious flavour it gives to the crust, while margarine gives a lighter pastry, albeit with less flavour. It is possible to use a combination of the two for shortcrust pastries, but we wouldn't recommend anything but butter for layered pastries.

Lard was traditionally used in pastry making as it makes a wonderfully flaky crust, and we would still use it occasionally, such as when making meat pies. However, health concerns over animal fats in our diet has made the use of lard much less popular in domestic cooking. Vegetable shortening can be used as a vegetarian substitute for lard.

Some speciality pastries use oil or cream cheese rather than a hard fat, but generally recipes call for fat that is solid at room temperature.

FLOUR

Most flours contain gluten, which develops into a stretchy, elastic substance when it comes into contact with water and is worked by hand or machine. You need a little of this development to happen to ensure the dough holds together when it is cooked and to make it manageable when you are trying to roll and shape it. But too much gluten development means the dough will be tough and quite unpleasant to eat, in a 'cardboardy' kind of way!

White plain flour is generally the best flour for making standard pastries, as it is lower in gluten than strong flours and therefore better suited to producing delicious, tender pastry.

Brown plain flour can often be substituted for white, but it is much more absorbent, meaning you need to add more water to bring the dough together, and it can produce rather a tough pastry as a result. Using half white and half brown flour can be a good compromise between texture and fibre.

Gluten-free flour pastries often include xanthan gum, as it helps to hold the pastry together by mimicking the effects of gluten.

LIQUID

Water is used to make the most basic pastry doughs. Eggs also have the ability to bind the dough together as well as adding richness and colour. There are many recipes (not in this book) where acidity is added in the form of lemon juice or vinegar as it tenderises the pastry, but we have found the effect to be minimal and don't tend to include it.

SALT AND SUGAR

Salt and sugar are used to add flavour to a dough. A pinch of salt even improves the flavour of a sweet pastry; but their impact is greater than this alone. Both salt and sugar help the pastry to achieve a lovely golden colour as it cooks.

Sugar restricts the formation of gluten (see page 6), so a sweet pastry is rather more forgiving than a savoury one and will tend to be short and delicious even if it has been somewhat roughly treated.

You will need to adjust the amount of salt that you add to a pastry, depending on the saltiness of the butter you are using. While we use salted butter for many of our shortcrust pastries, they will also work well made with unsalted butter and an extra pinch of salt added with the flour.

Keeping pastry cool

With most pastries, including all short and layered pastries, it is essential to keep the pastry cool as you make it, to prevent the butter melting before it is properly incorporated. Yes, it helps if you have naturally cool hands – people who do certainly start with an advantage when making all sorts of short and layered pastries. But there are lots of tips to help those with warmer hands limit the time they spend with their fingers in the dough, which will warm up the fats.

Working with cool ingredients in a cool kitchen really helps, but using knives or a food processor or mixer to start working the butter into the flour can also stop the dough warming up and becoming greasy.

Pastry chefs have a reputation for military organisation, which makes sense, as having all the ingredients and equipment organised before you start will enable you to work swiftly and efficiently, giving the fat no time to melt into the flour.

CHILLING PASTRY

When you are making pastry, you need the fat to soften and be incorporated into the flour. However, the heat of your hands and the ambient temperature of the kitchen can cause the fat to melt too much and become greasy. If this happens, pastry can be chilled for a few minutes at any stage of making.

Once the dough has been made, it should be chilled to allow it to firm up slightly, which will make it much easier to roll and shape. While the pastry chills, the gluten also relaxes, which means the pastry will be more tender and easier to shape. If you are in a rush, you can miss out this chilling stage by working quickly to make the pastry, thus preventing the dough from warming up too much; in this instance it can be rolled and shaped straight away. Alternatively, you can chill it quickly in the freezer, but take care as pastry that is too cold will be impossible to roll.

Wrap pastry closely in cling film when you chill it, to prevent the surface from drying out. Shortcrust pastry will need about 20 minutes to chill and rest; enriched pastries may take a little longer as they are softer to start with. Chill pastry in a disc shape rather than in a ball as it will make rolling out much easier and much less prone to cracking when you start to roll it.

The most important stage of chilling is when the pastry has been rolled out and is in its final shape before baking. The lined pastry case, the shaped tart or the pie lid must be cold and hardened before baking (choux, strudel and suet pastries are exceptions to this). If the pastry is not chilled, the butter will start to melt before the heat of the oven has set the flour into shape, and your pastry will simply slump and melt down the sides of the tin. If there is time, you should allow the pastry to get so cold that it is solid to the touch before it is baked; try to allow 20–30 minutes for chilling before baking. This can be done in the freezer if you are in a hurry.

When making layered pastries, the fat must be kept cool but still pliable throughout the process, to stop it melting into, or breaking through, the layers of dough, which would prevent the pastry from rising. Take the layered pastry out of the fridge about 15–20 minutes before using, to make sure the butter is flexible.

Most pastries can be frozen very successfully when raw, often with fillings in too, and then baked from frozen. This includes mince pies, which can be frozen raw in the tin.

1

SHORTCRUST PASTRIES

Shortcrust pastries have a tender crumbliness and are used in sweet and savoury recipes. The most important stage of the process is rubbing the fat into the flour properly. The fat acts as a waterproof coating around the flour grains, thus preventing them from absorbing too much liquid. In turn, this helps to stop the gluten in the flour developing, which would make the pastry tough. Once the butter is rubbed in, sufficient liquid is added to bring the pastry together, but not too much or it will toughen the pastry.

Making a short pastry always involves a compromise between a tender, crumbly pastry and a pastry that contains more liquid and is easy to work with. A crumbly pastry may tear when you try to line a tin, but you can easily push torn pieces together and repair holes with pieces of uncooked pastry, patchwork style. The result should still be deliciously tender.

RICH SHORTCRUST PASTRY

MAKES enough to line a 24cm flan ring

250g plain flour
Pinch of salt
140g chilled butter

2 egg yolks
3–4 tbsp chilled water

Shortcrust is traditionally made with a combination of lard and butter. Lard lends a superior shortness but lacks the flavour of butter, so we generally use all butter.

1 Sift the flour and salt into a medium bowl.

2 Cut the butter into small pieces and add to the flour. Using 2 cutlery knives and working in a scissor action, cut the butter into the flour, keeping the 2 knives in contact. Using knives rather than fingers helps to keep the butter and flour cool.

3 Once the butter has been broken down to small pea-sized pieces, use your fingertips to gently rub the little pieces of flour and butter together.

4 Give the bowl an occasional shake to lift larger lumps of butter to the surface. The mixture should become a uniform fine, pale crumb with no visible lumps of butter. If the mixture begins to turn yellow, the butter is softening too quickly and you need to put the bowl in the fridge for 5–10 minutes to chill the butter.

5 Mix the egg yolks and water together in a small bowl with a fork until evenly combined. Add 2–2½ tbsp of the egg yolk mix to the rubbed-in mixture and stir with a cutlery knife, to distribute the liquid as quickly as possible (this will create flakes of pastry).

6 Pull some of the flakes to the side and feel them; if they are very dry, add a little more of the liquid to any dry areas of crumb and use the knife again. Don't be tempted to add too much liquid, as it can make the pastry tough. Once you think the flakes will come together, stop adding liquid.

7 Use the flat of the knife to bring a few of the flakes and dry crumb together, to create larger lumps. At this stage the pastry should be uniform in colour, not streaky. Continue like this until there are no dry crumbs in the bottom of the bowl.

8 Pull the pastry together with your hands, shaping it into a flat disc, about 10cm in diameter and 1.5cm thick. Do this as quickly as possible, without overworking the pastry, which also makes it tough. Wrap the pastry in cling film and chill for 20–30 minutes before rolling out. This will relax it and prevent too much shrinkage, as well as firm up the butter.

Variations

✳ Rich herb shortcrust pastry Add ½–1 tbsp chopped herbs such as thyme, rosemary, oregano or sage, or 1 tbsp chopped chives to the crumb mixture before the liquid.

✳ Rich cheese shortcrust pastry Reduce the butter to 110g and add 30g finely grated hard cheese, such as Cheddar or Parmesan, before the liquid.

✳ Wholemeal shortcrust pastry Use wholemeal flour in place of plain, omit the egg yolk and use 80g butter and 45g lard. You will need a little extra water too.

✳ Plain shortcrust pastry For a less rich pastry, use 80g butter and 45g lard and omit the egg yolks. It may be necessary to add up to 1 tbsp extra water.

✳ Rich sweet shortcrust pastry Add 2–3 tsp caster sugar before the liquid.

1 Sifting the flour and salt into the bowl.

2 Cutting the butter into the flour.

3 Gently rubbing the fat and flour together with the fingertips.

4 Giving the bowl a shake to check the evenness of the crumb; any larger lumps of butter will come to the surface.

(Continued overleaf)

5 Adding some of the beaten egg yolks and water.

6 Using a cutlery knife to mix in the liquid and draw the pastry together.

7 Bringing the pastry together into a ball.

8 Wrapping the disc of pastry in cling film.

GLUTEN-FREE PASTRY

MAKES enough to line a 24cm flan tin

200g gluten-free flour
  (such as Doves Farm)
Pinch of salt
1 level tsp xanthan gum
40g chilled butter

60g margarine
1 tbsp icing sugar
  (for sweet pastry, optional)
1 large egg
15–25ml milk

We are lucky to have run classes with Tom Thexton of Wild Thexton, who supplies many of the best restaurants in London with his gluten-free bakes, and he has kindly shared his recipe for gluten-free pastry with us; it's the best we've tasted. It can be used like rich shortcrust pastry and baked blind if required.

1 Sift the flour and salt into a bowl with the xanthan gum. Cut the butter and margarine into small pieces and add to the flour. Using 2 cutlery knifes and working in a scissor action, cut the fat into the flour, keeping the 2 knives in contact.

2 Once the fat has been broken down to small pea-sized pieces, use your fingertips to gently rub the flour and little pieces of fat together until the mixture resembles pale breadcrumbs of uniform size. Alternatively, use a food processor and pulse the ingredients to reach this stage. Stir in the icing sugar if making sweet pastry.

3 Mix the egg with 15ml milk, using a fork, until evenly combined. Stir the liquid into the flour mixture and distribute as quickly as possible with a cutlery knife. If the pastry is still too dry and won't come together, add the rest of the milk, little by little.

4 Use the flat of the knife to bring the dough together, then pull the pastry together with your hands and shape it into a flat disc, about 1.5cm thick. Wrap in cling film and chill in the fridge for 20 minutes.

5 Roll the chilled pastry out according to the recipe, between 2 sheets of cling film or baking parchment; this makes rolling out much easier as the pastry may be crumbly.

6 Chill the pastry in its final shape until very firm before baking. Bake at 180°C/gas mark 4 in the top third of the oven. It is cooked when the pastry has no grey patches and feels sandy to the touch.

A note on making short pastries by machine...

✳ Food processors and food mixers (of the Magimix/Kenwood/KitchenAid type) are very effective for the rubbing-in stage of pastry making. Add the flour, pieces of cold fat and any salt and flavourings, and process by pulsing the food processor or using a low speed on the mixer with the 'K' beater until the butter and flour have reached a 'breadcrumb' stage. Stop mixing before the dough clumps together or you won't be able to add enough liquid into the dough to hold it together when rolling it out and once it is cooked it will crumble. We would recommend you then remove the crumby mixture from the machine and add any sugar and the liquid by hand, according to the recipe; it is very easy to make the mistake of adding too much liquid or overworking the dough when you continue adding the liquid by machine.

ROLLING OUT PASTRY

First, make sure the pastry is the right consistency to roll. It needs to be pliable but also firm enough not to 'squidge' down as soon as the rolling pin is pressed onto it. If the pastry is too soft it will stick to the rolling pin and the work surface, so chill it sufficiently first. Pastry that has been in the fridge too long will be solid and it will crack when you try to roll it, so leave it out of the fridge until it has started to soften.

Marble is the perfect surface for rolling pastry, as it stays cool and is completely smooth. Stainless steel or smooth plastic surfaces are usually better than wood, with its textured surface.

It is often a good idea to 'ridge' the pastry before starting to roll it out. This helps to start flattening a cold pastry without tearing, and it keeps an even thickness. It also helps to preserve any layers in the dough.

Lightly flour the work surface and the rolling pin. It is better not to flour the pastry itself as it is easy to press too much flour into the dough and end up with a grey, dry crust. Move the pastry around slightly on the work surface between every few rollings to ensure it is not stuck, and use a palette knife to slide underneath and release the pastry if it sticks a little. Sprinkle a little more flour on the work surface if it has stuck.

Pastry often has to be rolled into a circle. Only roll straight, forwards and backwards away from and towards your body. Move the pastry circle round after a few rolls, 45° or so, always moving the pastry and not changing the direction of your rolling pin. This will mean the pastry is rolled evenly from all angles and not stretched one way and then the other, and therefore will set evenly without shrinking back in every direction when it bakes. Also by constantly moving the pastry, you are ensuring that it has not stuck to the work surface.

Don't turn the pastry over when rolling; just roll one side. The side that has been in contact with the rolling pin is the 'best' rolled side so can be used as the presentation side.

A good rolling pin is one that is long enough to accommodate the pastry width as well as your hands either side. At Leiths we prefer to use a straight rolling pin without handles to ensure even pressure.

Pastry can also be rolled out between two sheets of cling film or silicone paper or baking parchment, which can then be peeled off before use. This is particularly useful when pastry is crumbly and prone to falling apart when being rolled out.

1 First 'ridge' the pastry disc: hold the rolling pin in both hands loosely and tap it lightly over the entire surface of the pastry a few times. Turn the pastry 45° and ridge again. Repeat until the circle has at least doubled in size. Don't turn the pastry over; it is unnecessary and can result in overworking.

2 Once the circle has at least doubled in size, start to roll it. Use 3 short, sharp strokes of the rolling pin, rather than one long roll. Turn the pastry 45° after every few rolls.

A note on ridging...

✳ Ridging is much gentler on the pastry than rolling, so continue to ridge as long as possible before starting to roll. If the pastry starts to crack a little at the edges, stop ridging and seal the crack with your fingertips.

A note on rolling...

✳ Use a loose grip on the rolling pin and avoid applying too much pressure when the rolling pin comes into contact with the pastry; you just need a light pressure to encourage the pastry gently to expand, not stretch. Also be aware that your dominant hand may push down a little more firmly than your other hand; even pressure is important for the end result.

3 Once the pastry is rolled to the required thickness (usually about 3mm), the pastry should be an even thickness and circular in shape with no excessive cracking at the edges.

LINING A FLAN TIN OR RING

We recommend using a loose-based metal flan tin or flan ring (without a base) for any pastry case that needs to be removed from the tin before serving. It is possible to use a solid metal tin, but it can be tricky to remove more delicate pastry cases; crossing 2 long strips of foil on the base of the tin makes it easier to lift the pastry case out.

Try to fit the pastry into the flan tin without stretching it. Pastry can be quite elastic, so if you pull it in one direction when lining the tin it is likely to pull back in the other direction while it cooks, resulting in an unexpected final shape! Also make sure the pastry goes right into the corners of the tin or it will fall into them as it bakes, again giving a very uneven edge.

1 Roll the pastry to a circle large enough to line the bottom and sides of the flan tin or ring. You can work out the diameter of pastry needed by measuring the tin or ring from side to side with a piece of string and checking this against the rolled out pastry. However, with practice it is easy to measure by eye.

2 Carefully wrap the pastry once over the rolling pin to support it and place it over the flan tin or ring set on a baking sheet, with the side of the pastry that was uppermost when rolling now against the baking sheet.

3 Gently lift the overhanging pastry up a little, encouraging the pastry inside the tin or ring to fit snugly, right down to the corners. Now start to lift the edges of the pastry out and over the edge of the tin or ring.

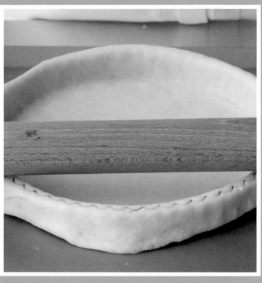

4 Tear a small piece of pastry from the excess and use it to push the pastry well into the corners. (You could use the side of your knuckle instead.) Ensure the pastry is smoothed up the sides of the flan tin or ring and folded over the edge.

5 Using a rolling pin and starting from the middle of the flan tin or ring, roll away from you and cut through the pastry, removing the excess. Turn the baking sheet around and repeat. Wrap any leftover pastry and trimmings in cling film and chill.

A note on lining...

✳ Avoid stretching and pulling the pastry as you line the flan tin or ring. Note that it is important to get the pastry well into the corners, or it will fall into them as it bakes and cause uneven shrinkage around the top edge.

6 Working your way around the edge with your thumbnail, release the pastry a little from the flan tin or ring, then neaten and smooth the top rim of pastry. Cover the pastry closely with cling film and chill until ready to use.

BAKING PASTRY BLIND

A pastry case often needs longer to bake than the filling inside, so to make sure both are perfectly cooked, the pastry is baked (i.e. blind baked), so that it is dry and set before the filling is added.

The pastry is first covered with greaseproof paper and baking beans which stop it over-browning and prevent the base from rising up and the sides collapsing during this first cooking. The paper and baking beans are removed before the pastry is returned to the oven to dry out a little before the filling is added.

The pastry case should be chilled before blind baking, and the oven preheated to 200°C/gas mark 6.

1 Cut a round of greaseproof paper (a cartouche), 8–10cm bigger than the tart tin. Scrunch it up, then unfold it and use to line the pastry case. Add a layer of dried beans or ceramic baking beans and fold the edge of the paper over the edge of the flan ring.

2 Bake for 15–20 minutes in the top third of the oven until the sides are set. To check, out of the oven, lift the paper away from the pastry. If the sides are holding up and the pastry looks less translucent and grey, remove the beans and paper.

3 Return the pastry to a lower shelf of the oven for about 5 minutes, or until the base of the pastry looks dry and feels sandy to touch, but has not taken on any colour. Remove from the oven and allow to cool slightly before using.

A note on baking blind...

The dried (or special-purpose ceramic) beans help to support the sides and edges of the flan case and weigh down the base to prevent it from rising in the oven. Scrunching up the paper first, before unfolding it, helps to get it into the edges of the pastry case, ensuring the sides are well supported by the beans.

Blind baking individual tartlets

If you bake small tartlets in bun tins (the kind of tin tray with 12 hollows, often used for making Yorkshire puddings) or small individual tartlet tins, it is easiest to use muffin cases to line them and to hold the baking beans, rather than having to cut out lots of circles of greaseproof paper.

Sealing pastry with egg white

To provide a protective seal between the blind baked pastry and a wet filling, so the pastry won't turn soggy, you can brush the pastry with lightly beaten egg white and return it to the oven for 3–4 minutes. This will also seal any very small holes.

A note on cooking pastry...

Pastry needs to cook at a high enough temperature for the pastry to set before the butter melts and runs out. In gas ovens, we would recommend most pastries are cooked in the top third of the oven.

Make sure the shelf is at the right height when you put the oven on to heat, as leaving the oven door open to change the shelves around just before cooking can mean a significant loss of heat.

Sweet pastries brown faster and more deeply than savoury pastries, as the sugar caramelises during the cooking process. Once the pastry has set into shape, it is often a good idea to lower the oven setting slightly for the rest of the cooking time, so the outside edge of the pastry is not over-browned by the time the middle is cooked, or to move the pastry to a lower shelf in a gas or non-fan assisted electric oven.

Repairing holes or cracks

If you are adding a liquid filling to a pastry case it must be watertight. After baking blind, check the pastry carefully for little holes at the edges or cracks up the sides, which can cause leakages. To repair these, soften a little of the leftover pastry in your fingers and plug the holes (as shown), or lay a strip of raw pastry over a crack, being very gentle with the pastry case. Return the repaired pastry to a lower shelf of the oven for 5–10 minutes to cook the raw pastry.

STILTON, FIG AND WALNUT TARTLETS

MAKES 24 small tartlets

FOR THE WALNUT PASTRY
120g shelled walnuts
250g plain flour
Pinch of salt
120g chilled butter
1 egg

FOR THE FILLING
4 eggs, plus 2 extra yolks
275ml double cream
125g Greek yoghurt
8 semi-dried figs
200g Stilton cheese
Salt and freshly ground
   black pepper

. . . .

Larger than canapés, these small tarts are ideal to serve with drinks before dinner, perhaps in place of a plated starter. Use a different blue cheese if you prefer. You will need two 12-hole shallow bun tins.

1 For the pastry, put the walnuts in a food processor and blend until evenly and finely ground, but still with a little texture. Sift the flour and salt into a large bowl. Cut the butter into small cubes and rub the butter into the flour (see step 3, page 12) until it resembles fine breadcrumbs. Stir in the ground walnuts.

2 Beat the egg in a small bowl. Add half the beaten egg to the walnut pastry mixture and mix well using a cutlery knife. Add more egg as necessary, until the pastry starts to come together in large flakes.

3 Using your fingertips, bring the pastry together. Shape into a fat sausage, roughly the same diameter as the tops of your shallow bun tray holes. Wrap in cling film and chill in the fridge.

4 To make the filling, break the whole eggs and yolks into a large bowl and beat together using a fork to break them up. Whisk in the cream and yoghurt until evenly combined, and season well with salt and pepper.

5 Chop the figs into 1cm pieces and crumble the Stilton into small pieces.

6 Remove the pastry from the fridge and slice off thin discs, 3mm thick. Use the discs to line the bun trays, pressing them into the edges and patching together where necessary to give a fairly even result. Try to ensure the pastry is no thicker than 3mm. Trim any excess from the edges and chill in the fridge or freezer for 15 minutes, or until very cold and firm. Meanwhile, heat the oven to 180°C/gas mark 4.

7 Blind bake the pastry cases (see page 20) for 12–15 minutes until crisp and golden around the edges. A little butter may foam around the edges of the pastry, which is fine. Remove the paper or muffin cases and beans and return to the oven for 2–3 minutes until the base is cooked through and sandy to the touch. Remove from the oven and lower the oven temperature to 150°C/gas mark 2.

8 Allow the pastry cases to cool slightly, then pour in the custard mixture until three-quarters full. Add the chopped figs and pieces of Stilton.

9 Return the tarts to the oven and bake until the filling is just set, with a slight wobble in the very centre, about 15 minutes. Remove and cool a little before un-moulding. Serve warm or at room temperature.

QUICHE LORRAINE

SERVES 6

1 quantity rich shortcrust
pastry (see page 12)
Extra flour, to dust

FOR THE FILLING
75g streaky bacon
1 medium-large onion
30g butter
3 eggs
350ml double cream
75g Gruyère cheese
Salt and ground white pepper

. . . .

This classic quiche is at its best cooked and eaten straight from the oven, or allowed to cool just to room temperature so the pastry is still crisp and the filling will be soft and smooth. You can make the pastry case a day in advance, but fill and cook it to serve. You will need a 24cm loose-based flan tin (or ring).

1 Roll out the chilled pastry on a lightly floured surface to a 3mm thickness and use to line the flan tin or flan ring set on a baking sheet (see page 18). Cover with cling film and chill in the fridge until firm to the touch, 20–30 minutes. Wrap and chill any leftover pastry. Heat the oven to 200°C/gas mark 6.

2 Meanwhile, for the filling, derind and finely dice the bacon. Halve, peel and finely dice the onion.

3 Melt half the butter in a small saucepan, add the bacon and sauté until golden. Remove with a slotted spoon and set aside.

4 Melt the remaining butter in the pan, add the onion, cover and sweat over a low heat until soft and slightly translucent (do not let it take on any colour). Drain the onion or remove the lid and allow the liquid to evaporate.

5 Blind bake the pastry case (see page 20) for 15–20 minutes, then remove the paper and beans and bake for a further 5 minutes, or until the pastry looks dry and feels sandy to the touch. Remove from the oven and reduce the oven temperature to 150°C/gas mark 2.

6 Put the eggs and cream into a small bowl and mix well with a fork until evenly combined. Pass this mixture through a sieve into a clean medium bowl. Grate the cheese.

7 Add the sautéed bacon and sweated onion to the egg and cream mixture with 50g of the grated cheese. Taste and season with salt and white pepper.

8 Using a slotted spoon, spoon the bacon, onion and cheese into the pastry; they should half-fill the case. Pour the rest of the egg and cream mixture over the filling, making sure the case is as full as possible. Sprinkle over the remaining cheese.

9 Carefully transfer the filled pastry case on its baking sheet to a shelf in the lower third of the oven. Bake for 40–50 minutes until the custard is pale yellow and just a little soft in the centre. To check, give the tart a little shake; there should not be a significant wobble in the centre.

10 Allow to cool slightly on the baking sheet, then remove the side of the tin, if using, and slide the tart onto a wire rack, or lift off the flan ring after transferring. Serve slightly warm or at room temperature.

. . . .

Variations

✱ For a lighter filling, replace half the cream with half-fat crème fraîche or milk.

✱ **Leek, mustard and Gruyère tart** Replace the onion and bacon with 2 small leeks (white part only), halved lengthways and thinly sliced into half-rings. Sweat in the butter, as for the onion and add to the egg and cream mix with the cheese. Spread 1–1½ tbsp wholegrain mustard over the base of the baked pastry case before adding the filling.

CRAB AND CHIVE TART

SERVES 6

1 quantity rich herb shortcrust
pastry, made with chives
(see page 12)
Extra flour, to dust

FOR THE FILLING
2 eggs, plus 1 extra yolk
250ml double cream
100ml crème fraîche
150g white crab meat
½–1 tbsp chopped chives
Salt and ground white pepper

You can buy picked white crab meat to make this tart, but if you have a freshly cooked whole crab, feel free to stir some of the brown crab meat into the egg and cream mixture (in place of 1 tbsp or so of the double cream) for a stronger crab flavour. You will need a 24cm loose-based flan tin (or ring).

1 Roll out the chilled pastry on a lightly floured surface to a 3mm thickness and use to line the loose-based flan tin or flan ring set on a baking sheet (see page 18). Cover with cling film and chill in the fridge until firm to the touch, 20–30 minutes. Wrap and chill any leftover pastry. Heat the oven to 200°C/gas mark 6.

2 Blind bake the pastry case (see page 20) for 15–20 minutes, then remove the paper and beans and bake for a further 5 minutes, or until the pastry looks dry and feels sandy to the touch. Remove from the oven and reduce the oven temperature to 150°C/gas mark 2.

3 Put the eggs, egg yolk, cream and crème fraîche into a small bowl and mix well with a fork until evenly combined. Pass this mixture through a sieve into a clean bowl.

4 Flake the crab meat and add it to the egg and cream mixture along with the chopped chives. Taste and season with salt and white pepper.

5 Using a slotted spoon, spoon the crab and chives into the pastry case; they should half-fill it. Pour the rest of the egg and cream mixture over the filling, filling the case as full as possible.

6 Carefully transfer the filled pastry case on its baking sheet to a shelf in the lower third of the oven and bake the tart for 40–50 minutes until the custard is pale yellow and just a little soft in the centre. To check, give the tart a little shake; there should be no violent wobble in the centre.

7 Allow to cool slightly on the baking sheet, then remove the side of the tin, if using, and slide the tart onto a wire rack, or lift off the flan ring after transferring. Serve slightly warm or at room temperature.

Variation

✱ **Prawn and dill tart** Use fresh or frozen and defrosted cooked shelled prawns in place of the crab, and dill instead of chives.

A note on seasoning with pepper...

✱ We use ground white pepper in egg custards as freshly ground black pepper can look unsightly if not ground fine enough, but if you prefer the flavour of black and don't mind the visual effect, feel free to use that instead.

ASPARAGUS, SPECK AND PECORINO TART

SERVES 4–6

1 quantity rich herb shortcrust
    pastry (see page 12)
Extra flour, to dust

FOR THE FILLING
12 fine asparagus spears,
    or 6 thicker spears
120g Pecorino cheese

5 slices of 6-month aged
    Speck
1 egg, plus 2 extra yolks
250ml double cream
Salt and freshly ground
    white pepper
A few chives, to finish

Parmesan can be substituted for the pecorino, and Parma ham can be used instead of Speck in this tart. You can also replace the chives with parsley or basil. You will need an 11 x 35cm loose-based rectangular flan tin.

1 Roll out the chilled pastry on a lightly floured surface to a 3mm thickness and use to line the loose-based rectangular flan tin. Cover with cling film and chill in the fridge until firm to the touch, 20–30 minutes. Meanwhile, heat the oven to 200°C/gas mark 6.

2 For the filling, bend the lower end of each asparagus stalk until it snaps, and discard the lower woody ends. Trim the spears with a sharp knife so they are all the same length. If the spears are thick, peel off the skin from the lower half using a swivel peeler and cut them in half lengthways. Grate the Pecorino, tear the Speck into large pieces and set aside.

3 Bring a large saucepan of water to the boil and blanch the asparagus for 1 minute. Drain quickly and refresh under very cold water to stop the asparagus cooking and to fix the vibrant green colour. Pat dry with kitchen paper and set aside.

4 Place the flan tin on a baking sheet and blind bake the pastry case for 15–20 minutes (see page 20), then remove the beans and paper and bake for a further 5 minutes, or until the pastry looks dry and feels sandy to the touch. If it is starting to take on colour, move it to a lower oven shelf. Remove from the oven and reduce the oven temperature to 150°C/gas mark 2.

5 Put the whole egg, yolks and cream into a small bowl and mix well with a fork, then pass through a sieve into a bowl. Add 80g of the grated Pecorino, then taste and season with salt and white pepper (bearing in mind that Speck and Pecorino are both quite salty).

6 Pour the egg, cream and cheese mixture into the tart case. Arrange the pieces of Speck in an even pattern on top, leaving enough room for the asparagus spears. Place the asparagus spears in between the pieces of ham and scatter over the remaining Pecorino.

7 Carefully transfer to the lower third of the oven and bake for 20–30 minutes until the custard is pale yellow and just a little soft in the centre. To check, give the tart a little shake; there should be no violent wobble in the centre. (An overcooked filling will rise up and feel springy to the touch.)

8 Remove from the oven and allow to cool slightly on the baking sheet, then remove the tart from the tin and slide onto a wire rack. Serve slightly warm or at room temperature. Just before serving, finely chop enough chives to give about 1 tbsp, and sprinkle them over the top of the tart.

SWEET POTATO, CARAMELISED ONION AND SAGE GALETTE

SERVES 6

1 quantity rich shortcrust
   pastry (see page 12)
Extra flour, to dust

FOR THE FILLING
900g sweet potatoes
2 large onions
6 sage leaves
2 tbsp olive oil
15g butter

½ tsp English mustard
   powder
150g goat's cheese log
Salt and freshly ground
   black pepper

TO FINISH
1 egg
A few sage leaves
A little olive oil

This way of making a tart is much more relaxed than blind baking a tart case, and is great for a lovely rustic presentation. You can use this method with the other short pastries in this book to make tarts of any firm filling, savoury or sweet – try using mixed summer roasted vegetables, or apples and dates, for example.

1 Heat the oven to 200°C/gas mark 6. For the filling, peel the sweet potatoes and cut them into 2cm dice. Halve, peel and finely slice the onions. Finely chop the sage leaves and set aside.

2 Place the sweet potato on a baking tray and pour over the olive oil. Season with salt and pepper and toss until well coated. Roast for 20 minutes, or until the potato is cooked through and starting to brown, then set aside to cool slightly.

3 Meanwhile, melt the butter in a large saucepan, add the sliced onions and cook over a gentle to medium heat until soft. Add the mustard powder and a pinch of salt, increase the heat slightly and cook the onions until golden brown, stirring frequently to prevent them burning; this will take about 20–25 minutes.

4 Roughly mash one third of the sweet potato using the back of a fork, and add to the onion. Stir in another third of the sweet potato and the chopped sage, and season with more salt and pepper if needed.

5 Beat the egg with a fork, then pass through a sieve into a small bowl and set aside.

6 On a floured surface, roll out the pastry to a circle about 30cm in diameter and 3mm thick. Transfer to a baking sheet and spread the sweet potato, onion and sage mixture evenly over the pastry, leaving a 5–6cm border.

7 Crumble over the goat's cheese and scatter the remaining sweet potato on top. Fold the border over, pleating the edges to form a round tart with an uncovered centre, and brush the border with the beaten egg. Dip the extra sage leaves in oil and scatter them over the tart.

8 Bake the tart in the centre of the oven for 30 minutes, or until golden brown. Remove from the oven and leave to stand for a few minutes before transferring to a serving plate and cutting into wedges. Serve hot or at room temperature.

SMOKED HADDOCK AND WATERCRESS TART

SERVES 6

1 quantity rich shortcrust
  pastry (see page 12)
Extra flour, to dust

FOR THE FILLING
225g smoked haddock fillet,
  skin on
200ml milk

6 black peppercorns
1 bay leaf
Large handful of baby
  watercress
3 eggs
350ml double cream
75g Cheddar cheese
Salt and ground white pepper

This tart is full of flavour. The peppery watercress complements the smoked haddock perfectly. Serve with a simple watercress salad – just dress some extra leaves with lemon juice, olive oil, salt and pepper. You will need a 24cm loose-based flan tin (or ring).

1 Roll out the chilled pastry on a lightly floured surface to a 3mm thickness and use to line the loose-based flan tin or flan ring set on a baking sheet (see page 18). Cover with cling film and chill in the fridge until firm to the touch, 20–30 minutes. Wrap and chill any leftover pastry. Heat the oven to 200°C/gas mark 6.

2 Meanwhile, for the filling, place the smoked haddock in a saucepan, skin side down to protect the flesh from the direct heat. Pour the milk over the fish and add the peppercorns and bay leaf. Bring to a simmer over a gentle heat. Cover the fish with a piece of damp greaseproof paper and poach gently for 5 minutes, or until just starting to flake.

3 Remove the fish from the pan and discard the milk. Skin the fish and remove any pin bones, then flake it into large pieces; set aside to cool.

4 Blanch the watercress in boiling water for 30 seconds. Drain, refresh in cold water, then drain again thoroughly.

5 Blind bake the pastry case (see page 20) for 15–20 minutes, then remove the paper and beans and bake for a further 5 minutes, or until the pastry looks dry and feels sandy to the touch. Remove from the oven and reduce the oven temperature to 150°C/gas mark 2.

6 Put the eggs and cream into a small bowl and mix well with a fork until evenly combined. Pass this mixture through a sieve into a clean medium bowl. Grate the cheese.

7 Add the poached haddock and blanched watercress to the egg and cream mixture with the grated cheese. Taste and season with salt and white pepper.

8 Using a slotted spoon, spoon the fish, watercress and cheese into the pastry case; they should half-fill it. Pour the creamy egg mixture over the filling, filling the case as much as possible. Lift some sprigs of watercress to the surface, for colour.

9 Carefully transfer to a shelf in the lower third of the oven and bake the tart for 40–50 minutes until the custard is pale yellow and just a little soft in the centre. To check, give the tart a little shake; there should be no violent wobble in the centre. (An overcooked filling will rise up and feel springy to the touch.)

10 Allow to cool slightly on the baking sheet, then remove the side of the tin, if using, and slide the tart onto a wire rack, or lift off the flan ring after transferring. Serve slightly warm or at room temperature.

HAM AND PEA POT PIE

1 quantity rich shortcrust
    pastry (see page 12)
1 egg, to glaze
Extra flour, to dust

FOR THE FILLING
85g (1 small) onion
85g celery
500g cooked ham or
    gammon

6 sage leaves
30g butter
50g plain flour
Splash of white wine
    (optional)
700ml chicken or ham stock
60ml double cream
85g fresh or frozen peas
Salt and freshly ground
    black pepper

This comforting pie can be made a few hours ahead and kept in the fridge until ready to bake. Serve with plenty of seasonal vegetables. You will need a 1 litre lipped pie dish.

1 For the filling, halve, peel and finely chop the onion. Finely chop the celery and cut the ham into 2cm dice. Finely chop the sage and set aside.

2 Melt the butter in a large saucepan over a gentle to medium heat. Add the chopped onion and celery and cook until soft and translucent, stirring occasionally, then add the diced ham.

3 Stir in the flour and cook for 1 minute, then remove from the heat and gradually stir in the wine, if using, and stock, making sure each addition is fully combined before adding the next. Bring to the boil, then reduce the heat and simmer for 2 minutes. Pour in the cream and simmer for a further 3 minutes, stirring, until it reaches a thick coating consistency.

4 Stir in the peas and sage and add salt and pepper to taste. Pour the filling into the pie dish and leave to cool completely.

5 Beat the egg to break it down, then pass through a sieve into a small bowl and set aside.

6 Roll out the chilled pastry on a lightly floured surface to a 3mm thickness and just bigger than the pie dish. Cut off strips from the edge of the pastry to line the lip of the pie dish (ensuring there is still a large enough piece to cover the pie comfortably). Press the pastry strips onto the lip and brush with a little beaten egg.

7 Carefully lift the pastry lid over the filling and press the edges gently onto the rim of the dish, to seal. The pastry should be just touching the surface of the filling.

8 Using a sharp knife, trim away the excess pastry and crimp the edges (as shown on page 39). Cut a small hole in the centre of the pie for steam to escape, brush with the beaten egg and chill in the fridge for 20 minutes. Meanwhile, heat the oven to 200°C/gas mark 6.

9 Place the pie on a lipped baking sheet, glaze again with the beaten egg and bake for 30–35 minutes, or until the crust is golden brown and the filling is bubbling and steaming through the steam hole.

PEAR AND ALMOND TART

SERVES 6

1 quantity rich sweet
   shortcrust pastry
   (see page 12)
Extra flour, to dust

150g caster sugar
3 tbsp Poire William liqueur,
   or brandy
45g plain flour

FOR THE FRANGIPANE
150g blanched almonds
1 egg, plus 2 extra yolks
150g butter, softened

FOR THE PEARS
2 firm, ripe large pears
½ quantity warm apricot
   glaze (see page 153)

. . . .

You will need a 24cm loose-based flan tin (or ring).

1 Roll out the chilled pastry on a lightly floured surface to a 3mm thickness. Use to line the flan tin (or ring) set on a baking sheet (see page 18). Cover with cling film and chill in the fridge until firm to the touch, 20–30 minutes. Heat the oven to 200°C/gas mark 6.

2 Meanwhile, to make the frangipane, blend the almonds in a food processor to a very fine crumb (ready-ground almonds can be used but grinding the nuts yourself gives a better flavour). Beat the egg and extra yolks in a bowl.

3 Beat the butter in a separate bowl until very soft, then beat in the sugar, in 4 or 5 additions, until fully incorporated. Gradually add the beaten eggs, beating well after each addition. Stir in the liqueur, add the almonds and flour and stir well to combine.

4 Blind bake the pastry case (see page 20) for 15–20 minutes, then remove the paper and beans and bake for a further 5 minutes, or until the pastry looks dry and feels sandy to the touch. Remove from the oven and leave to cool. Reduce the oven temperature to 180°C/gas mark 4.

5 Spread the frangipane evenly over the base of the cooled pastry case. Quarter and core the pears, then thinly slice across the width of the pear quarters (not with the length) into small slices, keeping the slices together.

6 Take a sliced quarter of pear, fan it out a little and place it on the frangipane so the top end of the pear is at the middle of the tart and the pear extends to the edge of the tin in fanned

out slices, radiating from the centre like the spokes of a wheel. Arrange the remaining pear quarters in the same way to make 6 or 8 spokes. (You may not need all of the second pear or you may need to add extra slices from the remaining 2 pear quarters if you have 6 spokes.)

7 Press the pears gently into the frangipane a little. Bake in the middle of the oven for 30–40 minutes until the frangipane has risen a little, is pale golden and set. To check, insert a skewer into the middle; it should come out clean. Leave to cool slightly on the baking sheet, then remove the side of the tin and slide the tart onto a wire rack (or lift off the ring after transferring).

8 While the tart is still warm, brush only the pears with the warm apricot glaze. The tart is best served warm or at room temperature on the day it is made.

. . . .

Variations

✱ Leave the cored pears in quarters, or even halves, instead of thinly slicing them. Very firm pears can be poached first.

✱ **Apricot and almond tart** Replace the Poire William in the frangipane with Amaretto. Replace the pears with 500g ripe apricots), halved and placed cut side down over the frangipane.

✱ **Plum and almond tart** Replace the Poire William with rum and the pears with 4–6 plums, depending on size. Halve and stone the plums and place cut side down in the frangipane.

PEAR, HAZELNUT AND CHOCOLATE TART

SERVES 6–8

FOR THE PASTRY
225g plain flour, plus extra
    to dust
50g cocoa powder
140g chilled unsalted butter
75g icing sugar
2 egg yolks
2 tbsp chilled water

FOR THE PEARS
1 quantity sugar syrup
    (see page 152)
4 firm, just-ripe pears

FOR THE FRANGIPANE
150g skinned hazelnuts
1 whole egg, plus 2 extra
    yolks
150g butter, softened
150g caster sugar
3 tsp Frangelico
    (hazelnut liqueur)
45g plain flour

TO GLAZE
½ quantity warm apricot
    glaze (see page 153)

This tart uses a chocolate pastry, which works very well with the sweetness of the frangipane. The pastry can also be used to make an easy sweet canapé – cook in tiny tartlet tins and fill with flavoured cream. You will need a 24cm loose-based flan tin (or ring).

1 For the pastry, sift together the flour and cocoa powder, cut the butter into small pieces and rub into the flour mixture (see page 12), then stir in the icing sugar. Mix the egg yolks and water, and add three quarters of this liquid to the crumb. Mix together using a cutlery knife to create large flakes, adding more liquid if necessary, then bring together into a dough.

2 Press the pastry into a flat disc, wrap in cling film and rest in the fridge for 15–20 minutes. Meanwhile, heat the oven to 200°C/gas mark 6.

3 Roll out the chilled pastry on a lightly floured surface to a 3mm thickness and use to line the loose-based flan tin or flan ring set on a baking sheet (see page 18). Cover with cling film and chill in the fridge until firm to the touch, 20–30 minutes.

4 Blind bake the pastry case (see page 20) for 15–20 minutes, then remove the paper and beans and bake for a further 5 minutes, or until the pastry looks dry and feels sandy to the touch. Remove from the oven and set aside to cool. Reduce the oven temperature to 180°C/gas mark 4.

5 For the pears, bring the sugar syrup to a simmer in a medium saucepan. Peel, halve and core the pears, then immerse in the sugar syrup and poach gently until tender, about 15–20 minutes.

6 Meanwhile, make the frangipane. Put the hazelnuts in a food processor and blend until finely ground (if too coarse, they will not bind the frangipane). In a separate bowl, beat the whole egg and yolks together.

7 Using a wooden spoon or an electric whisk, beat the butter in a bowl for 2–3 minutes, then gradually beat in the sugar, in 4 or 5 additions, until fully incorporated. Gradually add the beaten egg, beating well after each addition. Stir in the liqueur, add the hazelnuts and flour and stir well to combine evenly. Spread the frangipane over the base of the cooled pastry case.

8 Drain the pears and arrange them cut side down on the tart, pressing them lightly into the frangipane.

9 Bake in the middle of the oven for 30–40 minutes until the frangipane has risen slightly, and is set and pale golden. To check that it is cooked, insert a skewer into the middle; it should come out clean.

10 Remove from the oven and carefully remove the tart from the tin. Allow to cool slightly, then glaze just the pears with the warm apricot glaze. It is best served warm to room temperature on the day it is made, but is still delicious the day after.

CLASSIC
APPLE PIE

SERVES 6–8

1 quantity rich sweet
   shortcrust pastry
   (see page 12)
Extra flour, to dust

FOR THE FILLING
1 Bramley apple
6 Golden Delicious apples
75–100g caster sugar
½–1 tsp ground cinnamon
¼ tsp ground cloves
50g raisins
2 tbsp plain flour

We have kept our apple pie simple, adding only raisins, cloves and cinnamon, but would recommend using a handful of blackberries in place of the raisins in the autumn and raspberries in the summer. You will need a 1.3–1.4 litre pie dish.

1 Roll out the chilled pastry on a lightly floured surface to a large circle, at least 2–3cm bigger than the top of the pie dish and about 3mm thick. Cut a strip of pastry from the edge of the disc, the same width as the lip of the pie dish. Chill all the pastry on a baking sheet for 20–30 minutes.

2 To make the filling, peel, quarter and core all the apples and cut into 5mm thick slices. Place in a large bowl and sprinkle with the sugar, cinnamon and cloves. Stir through the raisins, sprinkle in the flour and toss together to mix.

3 Heat the oven to 180°C/gas mark 4. Place a flat baking sheet on an upper shelf in the oven to heat up.

4 Put the filling straight into the unlined dish. Remove the pastry lid from the fridge. Press the strip of pastry onto the rim of the dish and lightly dampen with water. Lay the pastry disc over the apples, pressing the edge down a little on the rim of the pie dish to seal. Carefully trim off the excess using a sharp knife to neaten; save any trimmings for decorating the top of the pie.

5 Crimp the pastry edge (as shown on page 39). Make a steam hole in the centre of the pie and decorate with leaves or other shapes cut from the pastry trimmings, if desired. The trimmings should be rolled very thinly, to about 1–2mm, and stuck to the top of the pie with a little water.

6 Stand the pie dish on the hot baking sheet in the oven and bake for 35–40 minutes until the apples are hot and the pastry is cooked and golden in colour. To check that the filling is hot, test with a skewer through the steam hole.

7 Remove the pie from the oven and allow to cool slightly before serving, with custard, ice cream or pouring cream.

A note on using a pie funnel...

✱ If making a large single crust pie, to ensure the pastry is held up over the filling, it may be necessary to stand a pie funnel in the middle of the dish. This will support the pastry, holding it above the filling and helping to keep it crisp.

DOUBLE-CRUST CHERRY PIE

SERVES 6–8

2 x quantity rich sweet
shortcrust pastry
(see page 12)
Extra flour, to dust

FOR THE FILLING
1kg red cherries
2½ tbsp cornflour
100–125g caster sugar

This is a decadent use of cherries but worth it for the delicious red syrupy filling which bubbles inside the sweet pastry crust. Some supermarkets sell frozen pitted cherries which makes this a more affordable and year-round treat, but nothing beats fresh cherries if you are lucky enough to have them in abundance. You will need a 1.3–1.4 litre pie dish.

1 Cut the chilled pastry in half and reshape into 2 discs. Wrap one disc closely in cling film and place in the fridge. Roll the remaining disc on a lightly floured surface to a large circle, 2–3mm thick. Use it to line a 24cm pie dish and carefully trim off the excess using a sharp knife. Save any trimmings for decorating the top of the pie. Cover with cling film and place in the fridge to chill for 20–30 minutes.

2 Roll out the second disc into a large circle, big enough to cover the pie, about 2–3mm thick, and place on a baking sheet. Cover with cling film and place in the fridge to chill.

3 To make the filling, remove the stones from the cherries, using a cherry stoner, then place in a large bowl and sprinkle with the cornflour and sugar. Toss together to mix.

4 Heat the oven to 200°C/gas mark 6. Place a flat baking sheet on a lower shelf in the oven to provide 'bottom heat'.

5 Remove the pie case from the fridge and fill generously with the cherry filling.

6 Remove the pastry lid from the fridge. Brush the rim of the pie case with a little water and place the pastry lid on top of the cherries, pressing down a little on the edge of the pie dish to seal the pastry.

7 Trim the pastry edges to neaten, then crimp the edge (as shown on page 39). Make a steam hole in the centre of the pie and decorate with pastry trimmings, if desired. The trimmings should be rolled very thinly, to about 1–2mm, and stuck to the top of the pie with a little water.

8 Stand the pie dish on the hot baking sheet in the oven and bake for 30 minutes to cook the bottom pastry before the top browns too much. Lower the oven setting to 180°C/gas mark 4, transfer the pie on its baking sheet to the top third of the oven and continue to cook until the pastry is golden and the filling hot. Test with a skewer through the steam hole.

9 Remove the pie from the oven and allow to cool slightly before serving, with custard, ice cream or pouring cream.

PLUM AND RHUBARB PIE

SERVES 6

FOR THE WHOLEMEAL PASTRY
170g wholemeal flour, plus extra to dust
Generous pinch of salt
25g lard
60g chilled butter
2 tbsp chilled water

FOR THE FILLING
500g small plums
½ tsp ground cinnamon
3–6 tbsp demerara sugar, to taste
250g rhubarb (3–4 small sticks)
2–3 tbsp caster sugar, to finish

This recipe uses wholemeal pastry and includes a little lard, for shortness. The wholemeal flour lends a lovely nuttiness, but you can use half plain/half wholemeal if you prefer. If the plums are large or not very ripe they should be cooked in a little sugar syrup first. You will need a 1.3–1.4 litre rectangular pie dish.

1 For the pastry, sift the flour and salt into a large bowl. Cut the fats into the flour, then use your fingertips to rub the flour and fat together, giving the bowl an occasional shake to lift the larger lumps of fat to the surface (see page 12).

2 Add 1½ tbsp of the water and use a cutlery knife to distribute as quickly as possible, creating flakes of pastry. Pull some of the flakes to the side and feel them; if they are very dry, add a little more water to any dry areas of crumb and use the knife again.

3 Use the flat of the knife to bring a few of the flakes and dry crumb together, creating larger lumps. Continue like this until there are no dry crumbs left in the bottom of the bowl.

4 Pull the pastry together with your hands, shaping it into a flat disc, about 10cm in diameter and about 1.5cm thick, working as quickly as possible to avoid the pastry becoming tough. Wrap in cling film and chill in the fridge for 20–30 minutes. Heat the oven to 200°C/gas mark 6.

5 Meanwhile, to prepare the filling, halve and stone the plums, then place in a large bowl with the cinnamon and demerara sugar. Cut the rhubarb into 2cm pieces and add to the bowl. Toss everything together to coat the fruit and tip into the pie dish; the fruit should come up to the rim.

6 Roll out the chilled pastry on a lightly floured surface to a 3–4mm thickness and about 5cm bigger than the top of the pie dish.

7 Cut a strip of pastry from each edge, the same width as the rim of the dish (as shown). Press the strips onto the rim of the pie dish, sealing the joins. Brush lightly with water (as shown) and place the rolled-out pastry on top. Trim the edges using a knife and crimp them by pressing between the forefingers and thumb (as shown).

8 Shape leaves or decoration from the pastry trimmings, then brush the top of the pie with water and decorate with the pastry leaves. Brush the leaves with water and dredge the whole pie with caster sugar.

9 Cut 1 or 2 small slits in the pastry top for steam to escape, then place the pie on a lipped baking tray and bake on the top shelf of the oven for 30–35 minutes until the pastry is cooked and the fruit is tender; use a skewer through a steam hole to check. Allow to cool a little before serving.

A note on the cooking juices...

✱ The plums and rhubarb release a lot of juice. If you prefer more syrupy juices, add 2–3 tbsp cornflour to the fruit, which will help to thicken the juice.

2
ENRICHED PASTRIES

The ingredients may be similar to shortcrust, but the method for these French pastries is quite different and the dough created much softer, so calling for longer chilling time before baking.

Pâte sucrée tastes almost cookie-like due to the high sugar quantity and vanilla flavour of the dough. It needs to be carefully checked towards the end of the cooking time as it should be a pale biscuit colour rather than a golden brown, and must be removed from the tin while still warm or it will stick. All the recipes made using pâte sucrée or sablée can also be made with rich sweet shortcrust pastry (see page 12) if you prefer.

PÂTE SUCRÉE

MAKES enough to line a 24cm flan ring

250g plain flour
Pinch of salt
125g unsalted butter,
softened

125g caster sugar
4 small egg yolks
2–3 drops of vanilla extract

This is an enriched version of shortcrust pastry, with extra butter and egg yolks replacing the water. We use a traditional method of making pâte sucrée by hand, although it can be made in a food processor.

1 Sift the flour and salt onto a clean work surface and, using the side of your hand, spread the flour out into a large ring.

2 Place the softened butter, in one piece, in the middle and, using the fingertips of one hand, push down ('peck') on the butter to soften it a little more, but without it becoming greasy; it should be soft, but still cold. It is important that the butter is uniformly soft, as if there are still small lumps of cold, hard butter in the mixture they can cause greasiness and holes in the finished pastry.

3 Sprinkle over the sugar and 'peck' until the sugar is just fully incorporated.

4 Add the egg yolks and vanilla extract and continue to 'peck' until the egg yolk is fully incorporated and there is no colour streakiness.

5 Using a palette knife, flick all the flour onto the butter, sugar and egg yolks and, using the edge of the palette knife, 'chop' the flour into the butter and sugar mixture. This technique helps to keep the flour from being overworked. Use the palette knife to lift any flour left on the work surface to the top occasionally.

6 As you continue to do this, you will create large flakes of pastry. Continue until there are no obvious dry floury bits among the pastry; it should be a fairly uniform colour. Floury patches at this stage will mean having to overwork the pastry at the next stage to incorporate them.

7 Now shape the pastry into a long sausage and, using the palette knife on its side, scrape a little of the large flakes together at a time. This will finally bring the pastry together and is called 'fraisering'. As more pastry sticks to the palette knife, scrape it off using a cutlery knife to avoid overworking it. Continue in this manner until all the pastry is fraisered: one or two more fraiserings are possible, but the more you fraiser the more the pastry will be overworked.

8 Bring the pastry together with your hands to form a ball.

9 Now shape the pastry into a flat disc. Wrap well in cling film and chill for about 30 minutes to allow the butter to firm up before rolling out.

Making pâte sucrée in a food processor

✳ Place the softened butter and sugar in a food processor and pulse until fully combined. Add the egg yolks and vanilla extract and pulse again until fully incorporated. Now add the flour and salt and pulse quickly until all the flour has been incorporated into the butter, sugar and egg yolk mixture, and it has a uniform colour and texture. Remove from the food processor and bring the pastry together in your hands before chilling.

1 Spreading the sifted flour into a large ring.

2 'Pecking' the butter to further soften it.

3 'Pecking' the sugar and butter together.

4 Incorporating the egg yolks and vanilla.

(Continued overleaf)

5 'Chopping' the flour into the mixture.

6 Creating large flakes of pastry by 'chopping'.

7 'Fraisering' the pastry, using the palette knife on its side, to bring the large flakes of pastry together.

8 Gathering the pastry together to form a ball.

LEMON TART

1 quantity pâte sucrée
(see page 42)
Extra flour, to dust

FOR THE FILLING
3 lemons
6 eggs, plus 1 extra yolk
150–170g caster sugar
225ml double cream
Icing sugar, to dust

It is best to prepare the filling for this tart a day in advance, to enable the zest to impart more flavour, but if you are short of time, 2–3 hours will be sufficient. You will need a 24cm loose-based flan tin (or ring).

1 To make the filling, finely grate the zest of the lemons and squeeze the juice; you will need about 100–125ml juice. Put the eggs and extra yolk into a large bowl, add 150g of the sugar and, using a balloon whisk, mix well. Add the cream, zest and juice, and stir until combined. Cover and chill in the fridge for at least 2–3 hours, preferably overnight, to allow the flavours to develop.

2 Roll out the chilled pastry on a lightly floured surface to a disc about 30cm in diameter and about 3mm thick. Use to line the loose-based flan tin or flan ring set on a baking sheet (see page 18). Cover with cling film and chill until very firm to the touch, 20–30 minutes. Meanwhile, heat the oven to 190°C/ gas mark 5.

3 Blind bake the pastry case (see page 20) for 15–20 minutes, ensuring the paper is pushed well into the corners of the pastry and the excess paper is folded over the edge of the pastry case, to help prevent the pastry from browning. Remove the beans and paper, taking care as the pastry will still be very soft, and bake for a further 5 minutes. Remove from the oven and reduce the oven temperature to 150°C/gas mark 2.

4 Taste the filling. If it seems too sharp, add some or all of the remaining sugar, to taste. Strain into a jug and pour the filling into the pastry case, filling it about half full. Transfer the tart to the oven and pour in more filling until the tart is as full as possible. Bake for 40–50 minutes until almost set, with a very soft wobble across the surface. A violent ripple across the middle of the filling indicates it is not set.

5 Take the tart out of the oven as soon as the filling is set, allow it to cool a little, then carefully remove the sides of the tin or flan ring. Leave to cool completely.

6 Dust the surface of the tart with icing sugar before serving. You can glaze the icing sugar dusting using a kitchen blowtorch if you wish, but take care not to burn the pastry.

Variations

❋ **Passion fruit tart** Replace the lemon zest and juice with the sieved juice of 8–10 passion fruit. If not juicy, add 1–2 tbsp lemon juice.

❋ **Lime tart** Replace the lemon zest and juice with the finely grated zest and juice of 4–5 limes.

ELDERFLOWER CUSTARD TART

SERVES 6

1 quantity pâte sucrée
  (see page 42)
Extra flour, to dust

FOR THE FILLING
10 egg yolks
300ml double cream
300ml good quality undiluted
  elderflower cordial
30g caster sugar

This is a rich and decadent tart that works well served with a gooseberry compote or fresh summer berries. It does use a lot of egg yolks, but if you prefer you can use 3 whole eggs and 4 extra yolks instead – or make a batch of meringues with the egg whites! You will need a 24cm loose-based flan tin (or ring).

1 Roll out the chilled pastry on a lightly floured surface to a 3mm thickness and use to line the loose-based flan tin or flan ring set on a baking sheet (see page 18). Cover with cling film and chill in the fridge until very firm to the touch, 20–30 minutes. Meanwhile, heat the oven to 190°C/gas mark 5.

2 Blind bake the pastry case (see page 20) for 15–20 minutes, ensuring the paper is pushed well into the corners of the pastry and the excess paper is folded over the edge of the pastry case, to help prevent it from browning. Remove the beans and the paper, taking care as the pastry will still be very soft, and bake for a further 5 minutes. Remove from the oven and reduce the oven temperature to 150°C/gas mark 2.

3 Meanwhile, to make the filling, mix all the ingredients together in a large bowl, then pass through a sieve into a jug and refrigerate until needed.

4 When the pastry is cooked, pour in enough of the filling to half fill the pastry case. Transfer to a baking tray and place in the oven, then pour in more filling until the tart is as full as possible. Bake for 40–50 minutes until almost set, with a very soft wobble across the surface. A violent ripple across the middle indicates it is not set.

5 Take the tart out of the oven, allow it to cool a little, then carefully remove the sides of the flan tin or ring. Leave to cool completely before serving.

A note on elderflower cordial...

✳ It is important that the elderflower cordial used is of a sufficient strength. Check the directions on the bottle, which should suggest diluting 1 part cordial to 10 parts water or thereabouts. A weaker cordial will not give the required flavour.

PRUNE COMPOTE CUSTARD TART

SERVES 6

1 quantity pâte sucrée
(see page 42)
Extra flour, to dust

FOR THE FILLING
400g dried stoneless prunes
2 Earl Grey tea bags
500ml double cream
1 vanilla pod
9 egg yolks
100–125g caster sugar

This is a delicious take on a classic French tart. You could use almost any thick compote instead of prunes; apricots and dates also work beautifully. You can use 3 whole eggs and 3 additional yolks instead of the 9 egg yolks if you prefer a custard that is less rich. You will need a deep 24cm loose-based flan tin (or ring).

1 Put the prunes and tea bags in a small bowl and pour over enough boiling water to cover. Set aside for 20 minutes, or until softened slightly.

2 Roll out the chilled pastry on a lightly floured surface to a 3mm thickness and use to line the deep, loose-based flan tin or flan ring set on a baking sheet (see page 18). Cover with cling film and chill in the fridge until very firm to the touch, 20–30 minutes. Meanwhile, heat the oven to 190°C/gas mark 5.

3 Blind bake the pastry case (see page 20) for 15–20 minutes, ensuring the paper is pushed well into the corners of the pastry and the excess paper is folded over the edge of the pastry case, to help prevent the pastry from browning. Remove the beans and paper, taking care as the pastry will still be very soft, and bake for a further 5 minutes. Remove from the oven and reduce the oven temperature to 150°C/gas mark 2.

4 Meanwhile, drain the prunes well, discarding the tea bags, then transfer them to a food processor and pulse to a coarse, soft paste that holds its shape. If it's too loose, simmer to reduce in a small saucepan, then leave to cool completely.

5 Pour the cream into a medium saucepan. Split the vanilla pod in half lengthways, scrape out the seeds and add both the seeds and empty pod to the cream. Bring to scalding point (when small bubbles begin to form at the edges of the pan and the cream steams), then remove from the heat and leave to infuse for about 20 minutes, before removing the vanilla pod.

6 Put the egg yolks in a medium bowl, add 100g sugar and stir thoroughly with a wooden spoon to break up the yolks. Pour over a little of the infused cream to loosen, stirring constantly, then add the remaining cream in stages. Pass through a sieve into a large jug and taste, adding more sugar if necessary.

7 Spread a layer, 3–4mm thick, of the prune compote onto the base of the tart case. Over the back of a spoon, carefully pour on enough of the filling to half fill the pastry case. Transfer to a baking tray and place in the oven, then pour in more filling until the tart is as full as possible. Bake for 40–50 minutes until almost set, with a very soft wobble across the surface. A violent ripple across the middle indicates it is not set.

8 Remove the tart from the oven and allow it to cool a little, then carefully remove the sides of the tin or ring. Leave to cool completely before serving.

INDIVIDUAL FRUIT TARTS WITH ALMOND CREAM

MAKES 8

1 quantity pâte sucrée
   (see page 42)
Extra flour, to dust
Selection of summer berries
   or seasonal fruit such as
   plums, segmented oranges,
   peaches or apricots
1 quantity warm apricot glaze
   (see page 153)

FOR THE ALMOND CREAM
300ml milk
2 eggs
50g caster sugar
15g plain flour
20g cornflour
2 tbsp ground almonds
2 tbsp double cream
1 tbsp Kirsch

You will need eight 12cm loose-based individual tart tins. For even smaller tarts, you can use barquette moulds; these require a little more care in the lining, baking blind and removing from the tins.

1 Divide the pastry into 8 equal pieces and shape into flat discs. Cover all but one of the discs with cling film and place these in the fridge.

2 On a lightly floured surface, roll out the pastry disc to a circle, 2mm thick and about 15cm in diameter, and use to line a 12cm diameter loose-based tart tin (see page 18). Place in the fridge and repeat with the remaining discs of pastry, chilling all the cases until completely firm to the touch, 20–30 minutes. Meanwhile, heat the oven to 190°C/gas mark 5.

3 Blind bake the pastry cases (see page 21) for 15 minutes, ensuring the paper is pressed well into the corners of the pastry and the excess is folded over the edge of the pastry case, to prevent the pastry from browning.

4 Check the sides are set and the base cooked through a little, then carefully remove the beans and paper. The pastry is still very soft and thin, so handle it carefully. Return to a lower shelf of the oven for a further 5 minutes, to dry out completely, but without allowing the pastry to colour.

5 Remove the tart cases from the oven and allow to cool for 1 minute, then release each one from its tin while still warm (or they will stick as they cool down), being gentle as they are delicate. Transfer to a wire rack and leave to cool completely.

6 For the almond cream, pour the milk into a medium saucepan and bring to scalding point (see page 155) and remove from the heat. Separate the eggs, placing the yolks in a medium bowl and the whites in a larger bowl. Mix half the sugar into the yolks and then stir in the flours until well combined with no visible lumps. Pour on the milk a little at a time, stirring as you pour, until thoroughly combined.

7 Return the mixture to a clean saucepan and bring to the boil over a low to medium heat, stirring with a wooden spoon. It will thicken rapidly, so stir vigorously to beat out any lumps. Remove from the heat and scrape into a bowl to cool slightly.

8 Stir in the ground almonds, cream and Kirsch and cool completely. Lay a piece of cling film over the surface of the cream to prevent a skin forming. When cool, whisk the egg whites to medium peaks, add the remaining sugar and whisk again to stiff peaks. Fold this into the cooled cream.

9 Fill a piping bag fitted with a 7mm–1cm nozzle with the almond cream and pipe into the 8 tartlet cases as neatly as possible, so that it comes just below the rim of the pastry. Arrange the fruit carefully on each tart, covering the cream. Glaze the fruit, and not the pastry, with the apricot glaze.

Variation

✳ Individual fruit tarts with crème pâtissière Replace the almond cream with 1 quantity crème pâtissière (see page 152).

GREENGAGE TARTLETS WITH SABAYON

MAKES 8 tartlets

1 quantity pâte sucrée (see
     page 42) or pâte sablée
     (see page 58)
Extra flour, to dust

FOR THE GREENGAGES
16 ripe greengages
200g granulated sugar

250ml water
1 vanilla pod

FOR THE SABAYON
4 egg yolks
2 tbsp caster sugar
50ml Sauternes
50ml double cream

This recipe is a lovely way to present greengages when they are in season, but it also works well with other stone fruit such as plums, apricots and peaches. All the component parts of the dish (except the sabayon) can be prepared in advance and assembled at the last minute. You will need eight 10cm tartlet tins.

1 Line the base of 8 tartlet tins, 10cm in diameter, with small circles of baking parchment. Divide the chilled pastry into 8 equal pieces and reshape into flat discs. Cover all but one of the discs with cling film and return to the fridge.

2 On a lightly floured surface, roll out the pastry disc into a circle about 13cm in diameter and 2mm thick. Use to line one of the tins, cover with cling film and place in the fridge. Repeat with the remaining discs of pastry. Chill until completely firm to the touch, 20–30 minutes. Meanwhile, heat the oven to 190°C/gas mark 5.

3 Blind bake the individual pastry cases (see page 21) for 10–15 minutes, ensuring the paper is pushed well into the corners of the pastry and the excess paper is folded over the edge of the cases, to help prevent the pastry from browning. Remove the beans and papers, taking care as the pastry will still be delicate, and bake for a further 5 minutes until the pastry is cooked through but not overly coloured.

4 Allow to cool in the tins for 1 minute, then gently release the pastry cases from the tins (they will stick if left to cool down). Transfer to a wire rack and leave to cool completely.

5 Cut the greengages in half and remove the stones. Put the sugar and water in a medium saucepan and heat gently until the sugar has dissolved, stirring occasionally. Split the vanilla pod lengthways, scrape out the seeds and add these and the empty pod to the sugar syrup. Add the greengages and poach over a gentle heat until soft but still retaining their shape.

6 Remove the greengages from the heat and set aside to cool in the syrup, then as soon as they are cool enough to handle, peel off and discard the skins. Return them to the syrup and set aside to cool.

7 For the sabayon, put the egg yolks, sugar and half the Sauternes in a heatproof bowl big enough to sit over a saucepan of simmering water. Set the bowl over the pan, making sure the base is not in direct contact with the water.

8 Using a hand-held electric whisk, whisk the mixture for up to 10 minutes until it has increased in volume and is light and mousse-like. Remove the bowl from the heat and continue to whisk until the mixture is cool (this will take several minutes).

9 Meanwhile, in a separate bowl, whip the cream to soft peaks, then fold it into the sabayon with the remaining Sauternes. Chill until ready for use (but for no longer than a couple of hours otherwise it may separate).

10 Remove the greengages from the syrup and carefully spoon 4 halves into each pastry case. Top with a generous spoonful of cold sabayon and use a blowtorch to lightly caramelise the sabayon. Serve immediately.

CHOCOLATE AND PEANUT BUTTER TART

SERVES 8

1 quantity pâte sucrée
(see page 42)
Extra flour, to dust

FOR THE FILLING
175g smooth peanut butter
175ml double cream

175ml milk
Pinch of flaked sea salt
2–3 tbsp caster sugar
300g good quality dark
chocolate, at least 70%
cocoa solids
2 eggs, at room temperature

Here, the salt is an important, if unlikely, addition to the chocolate filling, which really accentuates the chocolate and peanut flavours. You will need a 24cm loose-based flan tin (or ring).

1 Roll out the chilled pastry on a lightly floured surface to a 3mm thickness and use to line the loose-based flan ring set on a baking sheet (see page 18). Cover with cling film and chill in the fridge until very firm to the touch, 20–30 minutes. Meanwhile, heat the oven to 190°C/gas mark 5.

2 Blind bake the pastry case for 15–20 minutes (see page 20), ensuring the paper is pushed well into the corners of the pastry and the excess is folded over the edge of the pastry case, to help prevent the pastry from browning. Remove the beans and paper, taking care as the pastry will still be very soft, and bake for a further 5 minutes. Remove from the oven and reduce the oven temperature to 150°C/gas mark 2.

3 For the filling, in a bowl, beat the peanut butter vigorously with a wooden spoon, then add enough water, about 1 tbsp, to give a spreadable consistency.

4 Bring the cream, milk, salt and 2 tbsp sugar to a simmer in a medium saucepan over a medium heat. Break or chop the chocolate into small pieces and put into a medium heatproof bowl. Pour the hot cream mixture over the chocolate and leave to melt, stirring occasionally until it is fully melted and combined. Taste and add more sugar if necessary.

5 In a separate bowl, break the eggs up gently with a fork, trying not to incorporate any air. Pass the egg through a sieve into the chocolate and cream mixture, stirring until the mixture is shiny and glossy.

6 Spread the peanut butter over the base of the cooked pastry case, creating a layer about 3mm thick. Pour the chocolate mixture carefully over the top, transfer to a baking tray and bake in the middle to lower part of the oven for 25–30 minutes until softly set, with a uniform wobble.

7 Remove from the oven and leave the tart to cool for a few minutes before removing carefully from the tin and transferring to a wire rack to cool completely before serving.

PINOLATA
(PINE NUT TORTE)

SERVES 6

1 quantity pâte sucrée
  (see page 42)
Extra flour, to dust

FOR THE FILLING
120g butter, softened
175g caster sugar

3 tbsp plain flour
2 eggs, plus 2 extra yolks
175g ground almonds
165g pine nuts
6 tbsp apricot jam or
  conserve

This version of the classic Italian tart was a great hit at the school when we tasted it with morning coffee. It would be the perfect finale to an al fresco lunch, served warm with crème fraîche. You will need a 24cm loose-based flan tin (or ring).

1 Roll out the chilled pastry on a lightly floured surface to a 3mm thickness and use to line the loose-based flan tin or flan ring set on a baking sheet (see page 18). Cover with cling film and chill in the fridge until very firm to the touch, 20–30 minutes. Meanwhile, heat the oven to 190°C/gas mark 5.

2 Blind bake the pastry case (see page 20) for 15–20 minutes, ensuring the paper is pushed well into the corners of the pastry and the excess paper is folded over the edge of the case, to help prevent the pastry from browning. Remove the beans and paper, taking care as the pastry will still be very soft, and bake for a further 5 minutes until sandy to the touch. Remove from the oven and reduce the oven temperature to 180°C/gas mark 4.

3 Meanwhile, to make the filling, put the butter in a lightly warmed bowl and beat with an electric whisk until light and creamy. Beat in the sugar and continue beating until the mixture is pale and fluffy. Sprinkle over the flour.

4 Beat the whole eggs and yolks together in a separate bowl, then beat into the creamed mixture a little at a time. Fold in the ground almonds and 50g of the pine nuts.

5 Spread the apricot jam or conserve over the base of the cooked pastry case, then spoon in the almond filling. Smooth the surface with a knife and sprinkle the remaining pine nuts over the top.

6 Bake for about 40 minutes, or until the filling has set and the top is lightly browned. If the top starts to brown too much before it is cooked, place a piece of foil over the tart once the pastry has coloured. If the middle still seems uncooked and the nuts are in danger of getting too brown, lower the oven temperature and cook for an extra 10–20 minutes.

7 Remove from the oven and leave for 5 minutes, before carefully removing the tart from the tin while still warm and transferring it to a wire rack to cool. Serve warm or at room temperature, with cream or crème fraîche.

CHOCOLATE AND SALTED CARAMEL TART

SERVES 8

1 quantity pâte sucrée (see
    page 42) or pâte sablée
    (see page 58)
Extra flour, to dust

**FOR THE SALTED
CARAMEL**
150g caster sugar
65ml double cream
20g unsalted butter
¼ tsp flaked sea salt

**FOR THE CHOCOLATE
FILLING**
300ml double cream
50g caster sugar
275g good quality dark
    chocolate, minimum
    60% cocoa solids
3 eggs, plus 2 extra yolks

For this wonderfully rich, decadent tart you will need a 24cm loose-based flan tin (or ring).

1 Roll out the chilled pastry on a lightly floured surface to a 3mm thickness and use to line the loose-based flan tin or flan ring set on a baking sheet (see page 18). Cover with cling film and chill in the fridge until very firm to the touch, 20–30 minutes. Meanwhile, heat the oven to 190°C/gas mark 5.

2 Blind bake the pastry case (see page 20) for 15–20 minutes, ensuring that the paper is pushed well into the corners of the pastry and the excess is folded over the edge of the pastry case, to help prevent the pastry from browning. Remove the beans and paper, taking care as the pastry will still be very soft, and bake for a further 5 minutes, or until the pastry is cooked through. Leave to cool briefly, then release the pastry from the tin or ring (or it will stick as it cools) and place on a baking sheet. Reduce the oven temperature to 150°C/gas mark 2.

3 To make the salted caramel, sprinkle the sugar over the base of a large saucepan; ideally the sugar should be no thicker than a few millimetres to ensure quick and even colouring. Place the pan over a low to medium heat and leave undisturbed as the sugar starts to melt at the edges. As more sugar melts and takes on colour, carefully swirl the pan to encourage even browning; you may need to use a wooden spoon or heatproof spatula to redistribute the unmelted sugar to the outside edges.

4 When all the sugar has melted, leave on the heat until the caramel has taken on a deep golden colour then, acting swiftly, pour in the cream, taking care as it will splutter and spit. Add the butter and sea salt. Allow to cool briefly before tasting and adding more salt if necessary. Set aside.

5 To make the filling, bring the cream and sugar to a simmer in a medium saucepan over a medium heat. Break the chocolate into a heatproof bowl, in small pieces. Pour the hot cream over the chocolate and stir until completely melted, then continue to stir until the mixture is shiny and glossy.

6 In a separate bowl, beat the whole eggs and yolks well with a fork and pass through a sieve into the chocolate mixture. Stir well, add two thirds of the salted caramel and continue stirring to fully incorporate.

7 Carefully pour the filling into the pastry case. In a swirling motion, pour the remaining salted caramel over the filling and use a small spoon to create a lightly marbled effect. Bake in the lower third of the oven for 15–20 minutes until softly set; it should have a uniform wobble; it will set more on cooling.

8 Remove the tart from the oven and allow to cool completely before serving at room temperature.

PÂTE SABLÉE

MAKES '1 quantity'

250g plain flour
Pinch of salt
200g unsalted butter, softened

100g icing sugar
2 egg yolks
2–3 drops of vanilla extract

Pâte sablée follows the same French pastry method as pâte sucrée, but by using icing sugar instead of caster, the pastry has a very tender, almost sandy, texture, hence its name (sablé is French for sand). It is a very soft dough and, unlike pâte sucrée, it often doesn't need fraisering (see page 42). When baking, as with pâte sucrée, try to keep the colour quite pale and remove from the tin or mould while still warm, to prevent it from sticking.

1 Sift the flour and salt onto a clean work surface and, using the side of your hand, spread the flour out into a large ring.

2 Place the softened butter, in one piece, in the middle of the ring and, using the fingertips of one hand, push down, or 'peck' on the butter to soften it a little more, but without it becoming shiny and greasy; it should be uniformly soft, but still cold (see step 2, page 42). It is important that there are no small lumps of cold, hard butter as these can cause greasiness and holes in the pastry.

3 Sprinkle over the icing sugar and continue to 'peck' until the sugar is just fully incorporated; it should be quickly absorbed.

4 Add the egg yolks and vanilla extract to the butter and sugar mix and continue to 'peck' until the egg yolk is fully incorporated and there is no colour streakiness.

5 Using a palette knife, flick all the flour onto the butter, sugar and egg yolks and, using the edge of the palette knife, 'chop' the flour into the butter and sugar mix (see step 5, page 42). This technique helps to keep the flour from being overworked. As you continue to do this, you will create large flakes of pastry. Continue until there are no obvious dry floury bits in the pastry; it should be a fairly uniform colour. Often sablée pastry does not require fraisering, as it will have come together though the chopping process.

6 Finally, bring the pastry together with your hands and shape into a flat disc. Wrap well in cling film and chill to allow the butter to firm up. Before chilling, the pastry is too soft to roll out and shape.

TECHNIQUE
PÂTE FROLLÉE

MAKES '1 quantity'

150g plain flour
100g ground almonds
Pinch of salt
150g unsalted butter,
  softened

100g caster sugar
3 egg yolks
2–3 drops of vanilla extract

Pâte frollée is made using the same technique as pâte sucrée, but the addition of ground almonds results in a more crumbly biscuity texture with a little less snap. Try using other ground nuts such as walnuts, pistachios or hazelnuts. Pate frollée can be used to make a flan case or biscuits. It also makes a lovely pudding when baked in simple discs, layered with lightly whipped cream and fresh raspberries and served with a raspberry coulis.

1 Sift the flour, ground almonds and salt together onto a clean work surface and, using the side of your hand, spread the flour out into a large ring.

2 Place the softened butter, in one piece, in the middle of the ring and, using the fingertips of one hand, push down, or 'peck' on the butter to soften it a little more, but without it becoming shiny and greasy; it should be uniformly soft, but still cold (see step 2, page 42). Check that there are no small lumps of hard butter as these can cause greasiness and holes in the pastry.

3 Sprinkle over the sugar and continue to 'peck' until the sugar is just fully incorporated.

4 Add the egg yolks and vanilla extract to the butter and sugar mix and continue to 'peck' until the egg yolk is fully incorporated and there is no colour streakiness.

5 Using a palette knife, flick all the flour and almond mixture onto the butter, sugar and egg yolks and, using the edge of the palette knife, 'chop' the flour into the butter and sugar mix (see step 5, page 42). This technique helps to keep the flour and almonds from being overworked. As you continue to do this, you will create large flakes of pastry. Continue until there are no obvious dry floury bits in the pastry; it should be a fairly uniform colour.

6 Finally, bring the pastry together with your hands and shape into a flat disc. Wrap well in cling film and chill to allow the butter to firm up. Before chilling, the pastry is too soft to roll out and shape.

WILD STRAWBERRY AND RASPBERRY SABLÉES

SERVES 4–6

1 quantity pâte sablée
(see page 58, prepared
to the end of step 5)
Extra flour, to dust

TO ASSEMBLE
3 tbsp freeze-dried
strawberries

1 small punnet of wild
or small cultivated
strawberries
1 small punnet of raspberries
1 quantity raspberry coulis
(see page 153)
Basil oil (see below), to finish

This is a different version of the French classic. If you can't get hold of wild strawberries, then just use the smallest you can find and cut them into halves or quarters accordingly.

1 Once the pastry has come together into large flakes of pastry (see step 5, page 58), sprinkle 2 tbsp of the freeze-dried strawberries over the pastry.

2 Bring the pastry together with your hands, making sure the strawberries are evenly distributed but without overworking the dough. Form the pastry into a flat disc, wrap well in cling film and chill for 10–15 minutes, or until firm enough to roll.

3 Roll out the chilled pastry on a lightly floured surface to about a 2mm thickness (the finished biscuit should be thin and crisp). Using a 10 x 6cm template, cut out 3 rectangles per serving and lay them on a baking tray. Alternatively, you can use a plain round 6–8cm pastry cutter to cut the same number of circles. Cover with cling film and chill in the fridge or freezer until completely firm to the touch, 20–30 minutes. It is worth making a few extra, as they are liable to break if not handled carefully. Meanwhile, heat the oven to 190°C/gas mark 5.

4 Bake the sablées for 6–8 minutes until evenly cooked and very pale with just the barest hint of biscuit colour. Remove from the oven and leave to cool on the tray for 1 minute, then carefully release them from the tray. While still hot, sprinkle the remaining freeze-dried strawberries over the tops, press down gently and transfer to a wire rack to cool completely.

5 Hull the fresh strawberries and fold them with the raspberries through half of the raspberry coulis, to coat lightly.

6 To assemble the sablées, place a biscuit on each serving plate and spoon a few strawberries and raspberries on top, making sure they are level, for the next biscuit to be laid on top.

7 Add another biscuit to each, then more strawberries and raspberries, and finally a third biscuit. Drizzle the remaining coulis around the plate. Finish with some drops of basil oil and serve immediately.

A note on basil oil...

✳ This is easy to make. Blanch about 20g basil leaves in boiling water for a few seconds, then refresh in cold water and drain well. Transfer to a blender, add 75ml each sunflower and olive oil and blitz until as smooth as possible. Transfer to a bowl, cover and leave to stand for a few hours. Strain through a muslin-lined sieve before using.

BERRY
AND ALMOND TART

SERVES 4–6

1 quantity pâte frollée
(see page 59)
Extra flour, to dust

FOR THE FILLING
1–2 tbsp rum, to taste
1 quantity crème pâtissière
(see page 152)

Caster sugar, to taste
(optional)
350g raspberries
350g blackberries
1 quantity redcurrant glaze
(see page 153), to glaze

If you are lucky enough to be able to find a more unusual mixture of berries, such as mulberries, loganberries and golden raspberries, try mixing them up, as the differences in colour and size as well as flavour make this delicious tart even more distinctive. You will need a 24cm loose-based flan tin (or ring).

1 Roll out the chilled pastry on a lightly floured surface, or between 2 sheets of cling film, to a 3mm thickness, and use to line the loose-based flan tin or flan ring set on a baking sheet (see page 18). As almond pastry is tricky to roll, you may need to patch the pastry together in the tin. Cover with cling film and chill in the fridge for 20–30 minutes or until completely firm to the touch. Meanwhile, heat the oven to 190°C/gas mark 5.

2 Blind bake the pastry case (see page 20) for 15–20 minutes, then remove the paper and beans and bake for a further 5 minutes, or until the pastry looks dry and feels sandy to the touch. Remove from the oven and allow to cool.

3 For the filling, beat 1 tbsp rum into the crème pâtissière. Taste and add more rum or a little sugar, if desired.

4 Carefully remove the pastry case from the tin and place on a serving plate. Pile in the crème pâtissière and level it out using a palette knife.

5 Pile the berries generously on top of the crème pâtissière, in a higgledy piggledy manner. Dab the redcurrant glaze evenly over the fruit using a pastry brush, making sure all the berries are covered.

PÂTE
A PÂTE

MAKES '1 quantity'

250g plain flour
½ tsp salt
170g unsalted butter,
   softened

2 egg yolks
2½ tbsp water

This is a savoury version of pâte sucrée that produces a very different flaky texture and a rich, buttery and delicious pastry. Not the ideal pastry to line a pie dish or flan ring, it is usually used to encase savoury fillings in a flat pie. It is essential to work some water into the pastry when making it, or it is very difficult to handle.

1 Sift the flour and salt onto a work surface and, using the side of your hand, spread it out into a large ring.

2 Place the softened butter in one piece on the work surface in the middle of the ring and, using the tips of your fingers on one hand, push down ('peck') on the butter to soften it a little more, but without it becoming shiny and greasy (see step 2, page 42). It should be soft, but still cold. It is important that the butter is uniformly soft, as if there are still small lumps of cold, hard butter in the mixture they can cause greasiness and holes in the finished pastry.

3 Add the egg yolks and continue to 'peck' until they are just incorporated into the butter. Add the water and continue pecking until combined.

4 Using a palette knife, flick all the flour onto the butter and egg yolk mixture and, using the edge of the palette knife, 'chop' the flour into the mixture (see step 5, page 42). This technique helps to keep the flour from being overworked.

5 As you continue to do this, you will create larger flakes of pastry. Continue until there are no obvious dry, floury areas among the pastry; it should be a fairly uniform, even colour. This pastry often does not need fraisering and will come together though the chopping process.

6 Bring the pastry together with your hands and shape into a flat disc. Wrap well in cling film and chill in the fridge to allow the butter to firm up before rolling.

ARTICHOKE AND SHALLOT PICNIC PIE

2 x quantity pâte à pâte
  (see left), chilled as
  separate discs
Extra flour, to dust
1 egg

FOR THE FILLING
5 banana shallots
3 x 400g tins artichoke hearts
  (750g drained weight)

1 garlic clove
120g Parmesan cheese
Small handful of tarragon,
  about 10g
40g butter
150ml double cream
120g breadcrumbs
Salt and freshly ground
  black pepper

The filling of this tasty picnic pie can also be used to make a delicious meat-free version of sausage rolls (see page 93; use half the pastry quantity and omit the fennel seeds from the top).

1 For the filling, halve, peel and finely slice the shallots. Rinse and drain the artichokes, then roughly chop. Peel and crush the garlic, grate the Parmesan and chop the tarragon.

2 Melt the butter in a medium saucepan and add the shallots. Cover with a damp cartouche (see page 155) and a lid and sweat over a low heat until soft and translucent. Add the garlic and cook for 1 minute, stirring. Add the chopped artichokes and cook for 5–10 minutes to soften slightly. Pour in the cream and increase the heat to reduce the sauce to a consistency that will coat the back of a wooden spoon, stirring often to prevent it from catching.

3 Add the Parmesan, breadcrumbs and tarragon, and season with salt and pepper (bearing in mind that the Parmesan is salty). Leave the mixture to cool (it can be made up to 2 days in advance and refrigerated). When cooled the mixture should be fairly firm.

4 On a lightly floured surface, roll one chilled pastry disc into a rectangle about 12 x 30cm, and the second slightly larger in length and width. Chill on baking parchment on separate baking sheets in the fridge for 20 minutes. Meanwhile, heat the oven to 200°C/Gas mark 6.

5 Using a fork, prick the smaller pastry rectangle all over and bake in the oven for 15–20 minutes until lightly golden and cooked through. Remove from the oven and allow to cool completely on the baking sheet.

6 Spread the cooled filling over the cooled pastry base, leaving a clear 2cm border around the edges. Lightly beat the egg using a fork and pass through a sieve into a small bowl, then brush the pastry border with the egg.

7 Place the larger pastry rectangle on top of the filling and press all round the border to seal the edges; try to avoid creating air pockets. Trim away any excess pastry and lightly crimp the border using the back of a fork, to further seal.

8 Use any pastry trimmings to decorate the pie and brush all over with the beaten egg. Chill until firm, 20–30 minutes.

9 Bake in the oven for 35–45 minutes or until the pastry is crisp and evenly golden. Serve hot or cold, as a starter or light lunch, in slices, with salad leaves in a mustardy dressing.

HAM HOCK, CAPER AND MUSTARD PIE

SERVES 6

2 x quantity pâte à pâte
(see page 64), chilled
as separate discs
Extra flour, to dust
1 egg

FOR THE FILLING
1 cooked ham hock
Small bunch of flat-leaf
parsley

150g Gruyère cheese
150g crème fraîche
1–2 tbsp wholegrain mustard,
to taste
Pinch of English mustard
powder
Pinch of cayenne pepper
1 lemon
2–3 tsp small capers, drained

Ham and parsley are a classic flavour combination and here the piquant flavour of the capers and mustard balances the richness of the cheese, ham and pastry. Bake this for a picnic, as the perfect alternative to a traditional pork pie.

1 Roll out one chilled disc of pastry on a lightly floured surface to a circle about 26cm in diameter. Transfer to a baking sheet and chill in the fridge. Roll out the second disc to a circle about 24cm in diameter, place on a second baking sheet and chill in the fridge for 20–30 minutes until firm. Meanwhile, heat the oven to 200°C/gas mark 6.

2 Bake the smaller circle of pastry for 20 minutes until golden and cooked through. Remove from the oven and leave to cool on the baking sheet.

3 Strip the ham from the bone and tear into small bite-sized pieces (you will need 250g). Chop enough parsley to give you 2–3 tbsp. Set aside with the ham.

4 Grate the cheese and mix with the crème fraîche and mustard in a small bowl, then add the mustard powder and cayenne. Finely grate the zest from half of the lemon and add to the mixture, to taste.

5 Spread one third of the crème fraîche and cheese mixture onto the cooked, cooled pastry base, leaving a clear 2cm border around the edge.

6 Mix the ham hock, parsley and capers together and scatter over the surface of the pie. Spread the remaining crème fraîche mixture over the ham hock and capers.

7 Break the egg up with a fork and pass through a sieve into a small bowl. Brush the pastry border with beaten egg and carefully lift the larger, uncooked circle of pastry on top of the filling; try to avoid creating air pockets. Seal the top and bottom edges together by pressing well, either with your finger or a fork, to make a pattern as you seal. Trim off any excess pastry with a sharp knife.

8 Brush the pastry with the remaining beaten egg and bake in the oven for 20–30 minutes until evenly golden and cooked.

9 Transfer to a wire rack carefully and allow to cool a little before serving. It is also delicious served at room temperature.

3

LAYERED PASTRIES

Layered pastries rise because hundreds of layers of dough, separated from each other by rich butter, are pushed up by steam as the pastry cooks. Puff pastry has the most layers and therefore the highest rise but is also the most difficult to make. At Leiths, we start by making rough puff pastry, which is easier but still allows our students to practise creating the layers. We then tackle flaky pastry which has more layers and rises higher, before moving on to puff pastry, which after all that practice feels much easier to master.

All layered pastries are created using a technique of rolling out and then folding the pastry to create the layers. The base dough, or détrempe, is quite soft and elastic, as the gluten has been developed enough to allow it to stretch and strengthen the layering between the layers of butter and to trap pockets of air.

THE LAYERING TECHNIQUE

You will need to begin with cold or chilled ingredients and equipment. An efficient rolling and folding technique with short, quick strokes helps to keep the butter cool between the layers, which is crucial for a good, even rise. Maintaining shape and a uniform thickness is also important for even rising. If the pastry feels as though it is warming up and becoming elastic through overworking, chill it in the fridge. This will help to keep the butter firm. By resting the pastry for a while, you are also helping to relax the gluten that has developed, which will make the pastry easier to roll.

The gluten development needed to strengthen the layers, protect the butter and help keep the layers separate does need to be limited and controlled, to ensure the pastry remains light, tender and does not shrink excessively.

The objective is to incorporate the butter into the layers of détrempe (the pastry base) as thinly as possible, without allowing the butter to become greasy or melt.

Layered pastry needs to be cooked at a high temperature, to encourage rapid expansion of the air trapped between layers to quickly separate and raise the layers, and to seal the butter into the pastry.

Once you have mastered the layering technique, you can make puff, rough puff or flaky pastry. The difference between these classic pastries is the quantity of fat used and at what stage the fat is incorporated, which helps to determine how high the pastry rises.

The layered pastries are generally interchangeable between recipes, with puff the richest with the highest rise and most defined, even layering, followed by flaky, then rough puff.

Layered pastry making guidelines

✻ Keep the ingredients cold at all times, particularly the butter and pastry, which should remain cold but pliable, when rolling and folding, and shaping. If the pastry warms too much, the fat will begin to melt and stick the layers together.

✻ Work efficiently, with an awareness of the temperature of the pastry. Two sets of roll and folds should take no longer than 5 minutes.

✻ The détrempe should be soft rather than dry, and should be worked sufficiently to make it smooth and uniform in colour, but not excessively.

✻ Develop an efficient ridging and rolling technique. Keep checking for straight sides and square corners. Avoid creating ridges at the ends of the pastry and rolling over the edges.

✻ Relaxing the détrempe, and the pastry between roll and folds, will prevent overworking, stretching and shrinkage. Relaxing in the fridge will help to maintain the cold but pliable quality of the pastry, but if the pastry is left in the fridge too long then the butter will firm up too much and may break through the layers when rolled again.

✻ When relaxing pastry in the fridge, wrap it closely in cling film to ensure it doesn't dry out and make a note of the number of roll and folds that you have done, as it's easy to lose track.

✻ Avoid rolling the pastry too wide or long – it will become too large to manage easily and will become too thin, which can destroy layering. Conversely, avoid leaving it too thick – in this instance, the butter will not thin out enough so the pastry will be too heavy to rise properly and will bake to a greasy mass.

ROUGH PUFF PASTRY

MAKES about 500g

250g plain flour, plus extra to dust	150g cold but pliable unsalted butter
½ tsp salt	100–120ml (6½–8 tbsp) chilled water

We find rough puff pastry the easiest layered pastry to master. It has only 4 roll and folds and all the butter is added to the détrempe in large cubes, which flatten down to help create the flaky layers as it is rolled. Good rough puff pastry will double in height when it is cooked. Like puff pastry, rough puff can be prepared in advance; the same guidelines apply (see page 84).

1 Sift the flour and salt into a medium bowl. Cut the butter into 1.5cm cubes and add to the bowl. Add 100ml cold water and, using a cutlery knife, mix together quickly and efficiently for about 15–20 seconds, turning the bowl as you stir.

2 The flour and water will form large flakes, some attaching themselves to the cubes of butter. Drag the large flakes to the side of the bowl and add more water, ½ tbsp at a time, to the dry flour and butter in the bottom of the bowl. Quickly stir again with the knife, to create large flakes, adding a little more water if necessary. You should not ideally add any more than about 8 tbsp water, or the pastry may start to toughen.

3 Feel the large flakes and, if there seems to be a good amount of moisture within them and the water is evenly distributed, pull the large flakes together with the butter and mould the pastry in your hands a little to bring the détrempe together.

4 Gather it into a ball; it should now be a homogeneous dough, with the butter cubes dotted throughout and no dry, floury patches; try to cover any exposed butter with flour and water. Overworking with your hands will cause the butter to soften too much and become greasy. Shape the détrempe into a block about 12 x 17cm and 2–3cm thick, wrap closely in cling film and place in the fridge to relax for about 20 minutes.

5 Remove the détrempe from the fridge, unwrap and place on a floured surface, with a short end facing you. Ridge gently, patting up and down on the détrempe, keeping the rolling pin parallel to your body. Try to keep the sides straight and the corners of the pastry square, using a palette knife or your hands, but keep hand contact to a minimum to prevent the pastry warming up. Keep ridging as much as possible, as it is better for the pastry than rolling.

6 Now roll with quick, short sharp rolls, gently encouraging the pastry to lengthen rather than applying too much pressure and stretching it. Avoid creating thick ends at the top and bottom. Roll back a little if necessary and avoid rolling over the top and bottom edge, as you will stretch the top layer and create uneven numbers of layers, which will result in uneven rising.

7 When the pastry is 3 times as long as it is wide, re-check the sides are straight and corners square, then fold the bottom third of the pastry up over the middle third and the top third down and over the bottom and middle third. Turn the pastry so the folded side is to your left. This is known as a 'roll and fold'.

8 Repeat the roll and fold, making sure the pastry is cold to the touch and the butter is not becoming greasy. If some butter breaks through on the surface, then scatter some flour over it, dust off with a pastry brush and continue. Two roll and folds should take no longer than about 5 minutes. Wrap closely, making a note of how many roll and folds you have done, and place in the fridge again to relax.

9 Repeat the 2 roll and folds again, wrap and chill again. If after 4 roll and folds the butter is still evident and streaky, you will need to do one more, but generally rough puff pastry has 4 roll and folds. Keep wrapped in the fridge until needed.

1 Quickly mixing the butter cubes and water into the flour with a knife.

2 Stirring a little more water into the dry flour and butter to create large flakes.

3 Feeling the large flakes to check that there is sufficient moisture within.

4 Bringing the dough together with the hands to form an homogeneous pastry.

(Continued overleaf)

5 Ridging the rested pastry gently with the rolling pin.

6 Rolling out the pastry, using short, sharp strokes, to lengthen it.

7 Folding and turning the pastry to complete one 'roll and fold'.

8 Dusting off excess flour (sprinkled onto any exposed butter).

STEAK AND GUINNESS PIE

½ quantity rough puff pastry
(see page 72)
Extra flour, to dust
1 egg

FOR THE FILLING
1 onion
3 tbsp olive oil
Handful of mixed herbs, such
as parsley, thyme, rosemary
and oregano

1kg beef chuck steak
450ml Guinness
½ x 400g tin chopped
tomatoes
1 bay leaf
2 tsp softened butter mixed
with 2 tsp flour (beurre
manié), if needed
Salt and freshly ground black
pepper

Although this recipe uses only a half quantity of pastry, it is much easier to make a whole batch, so use half and freeze the leftover. You will need a large pie dish.

1 For the filling, halve and peel the onion and cut each half into 4 wedges. Place in a medium flameproof casserole or ovenproof pan with 1 tbsp of the olive oil, cover, ideally with a cartouche (see page 155), and sweat over a low heat until soft and translucent.

2 Meanwhile, finely chop enough herb leaves to give 1–2 tbsp and set aside. Trim off any excess fat and sinew from the beef, then cut into 2–3cm cubes. Heat the oven to 150°C/gas mark 2.

3 Once the onion is soft, remove it from the pan and set aside. Now brown the meat in batches in the pan, using more oil as necessary and deglazing with a little water after each batch.

4 Return the onion to the pan and add the Guinness, tomatoes, chopped mixed herbs, bay leaf and some salt and pepper, and bring to a simmer. Return all the meat to the pan and add a little water if the meat is not covered.

5 Cover, transfer to the oven and cook gently for 2–2½ hours, or until the beef is tender. You should be able to cut through a piece of the meat with the side of a fork or spoon.

6 Remove from the oven and drain off the cooking liquid into a small pan. Discard the bay leaf, then taste and reduce the sauce, if necessary, until it lightly clings to the meat and has

a good concentration of flavour. If the sauce needs thickening, whisk in the beurre manié, a piece at a time, over the heat.

7 Add the beef back to the sauce and transfer to a lipped pie dish, ensuring the filling fills the dish generously. Use a pie funnel (see page 36), if necessary. Leave to cool completely.

8 Roll out the chilled pastry on a lightly floured surface to a rectangle about 3mm thick and 3cm bigger all round than the pie dish. Cut off strips that together will line the lip of the pie dish. Lightly beat the egg with a very small pinch of salt, using a fork, then pass through a sieve into a bowl.

9 Press the pastry strips onto the dish lip and brush with a little beaten egg. Carefully lift the pastry rectangle on top and press gently over the lip, to join the edges. Trim off the excess pastry and cut up the sides (as shown on page 103). Place 2 fingers lightly on the edge of the pastry and draw the back of a cutlery knife between your fingers and upwards, to create a scalloped effect (as shown on page 103).

10 Make a hole in the centre of the lid to allow steam to escape. Cut out leaves or decorations from the pastry trimmings, if desired, and stick to the pie lid with beaten egg. Glaze the pastry with the beaten egg. Chill in the fridge for 30 minutes to firm the pastry. Meanwhile, heat the oven to 200°C/gas mark 6.

11 Brush the pastry with beaten egg again. Bake in the top of the oven for 25–30 minutes, or until the pastry is well risen and golden and the filling is piping hot when tested with a skewer.

A note on making savoury pies...

Savoury pies can be made using any stew recipe and adding a pastry lid. Just make sure there is enough meat or vegetable piled up to hold up the pastry lid when it is assembled, and enough gravy or sauce to accompany the meat and pastry. It is always best to make the stew first and allow it to cool down completely before topping with pastry, or the pastry will melt before it sets in the oven. Savoury pies can be made in this way using shortcrust or any of the layered pastries.

QUINCE AND CORNISH YARG PASTRIES

MAKES 6	

1 quantity rough puff pastry
   (see page 72)
Extra flour, to dust
1 egg

FOR THE FILLING
1 small quince, about 300g
60g pecan nuts
20g unsalted butter

3 tbsp Marsala
2 tbsp verjuice (see note)
1½ tbsp runny honey
85g Cornish Yarg cheese
Salt and freshly ground
   black pepper

TO FINISH
1 tbsp sesame seeds

A delicious variation of traditional Eccles cakes for those who like a savoury/fruit combination. Ideal to take on a picnic, they can be also be made smaller as canapés. If quince are unavailable, substitute firm pears.

1 Roll out the chilled pastry on a lightly floured surface to a 3mm thickness. Using a plain cutter or saucer as a template, cut out 6 discs, 12.5cm in diameter. Place on a baking sheet, cover with cling film and chill in the fridge while you make the filling.

2 Peel, core and cut the quince into pea-sized dice. Roughly chop the pecans and set aside. Melt the butter in a small saucepan, then add the quince, Marsala and verjuice. Cook, uncovered, over a gentle heat for 10–15 minutes, or until the quince is tender when pierced with the tip of a knife.

3 Stir the honey and chopped pecans into the quince. Increase the heat and allow to bubble for a minute or two, or until almost all of the liquid has evaporated and the quince is beginning to caramelise. Season with salt and pepper, taste the mixture and add a little more honey or verjuice if necessary; it should be a good balance of sweet and sour. Crumble in the cheese and set aside to cool completely.

4 Remove the chilled pastry from the fridge and place 1 tbsp of the cooled filling on the middle of each pastry disc. Dampen the edges of the pastry lightly with a little water, then bring the edges up and around the filling and squeeze into a money bag shape, making sure the filling is completely sealed in. Trim away the excess pastry using scissors, cutting as close to the filling as possible without exposing it.

5 Turn the pies over and flatten a little with your fingers, or roll lightly with a rolling pin, just until the filling is visible beneath the pastry.

6 Cover with cling film and chill on the baking sheet in the fridge until firm to the touch, about 20 minutes. Meanwhile, heat the oven to 220°C/gas mark 7.

7 Using a fork, lightly beat the egg with a small pinch of salt and pass through a sieve into a small bowl. Brush the pies with the beaten egg and sprinkle with the sesame seeds.

8 Using scissors, make a large snip in the pastry on the top of each pie. Make a second snip across the first snip, to open up the pastry in a small cross and reveal a little filling.

9 Bake near the top of the oven for 20–25 minutes until the pastry is golden brown and cooked through, particularly on the underside; there should be no grey patches. The baking sheet can be moved to a lower oven shelf once the pastry has set, to prevent over-browning. Transfer the pies to a wire rack to cool and eat while still slightly warm or at room temperature.

A note on verjuice...

✳ This is a really useful cooking ingredient if you can find it. It is pressed, unripe fruit juice, usually apple, crab apple or grape, and has great acidity as well as a lovely fruity flavour. If unavailable, use a mixture of apple and lemon juice or dry white wine instead.

FLAKY PASTRY

MAKES about 500g

250g plain flour, plus
extra to dust
½ tsp salt

170g cold but pliable
unsalted butter
100–120ml (6½–8 tbsp)
chilled water

Traditionally, flaky pastry was made with lard as well as butter, but we now use all butter. The base dough is enriched with butter as well as cubes being rolled and folded in to create layers. Flaky pastry has 5 roll and folds and will rise a little higher than rough puff, but not as much as puff. Like puff pastry, it can be made ahead; the same guidelines apply (see page 84).

1 Sift the flour and salt into a medium bowl. Cut the butter into small cubes (about 5–7mm) and divide into 4 piles; add one pile, so a quarter of the butter, to the bowl. Using your fingertips, rub the butter into the flour until it resembles fine breadcrumbs (see step 3, page 12). Add 100ml chilled water and, using a cutlery knife, mix together quickly and efficiently for about 15–20 seconds, turning the bowl as you stir.

2 The flour, butter and water will form large flakes. Drag these to the side of the bowl and add more water, ½ tbsp at a time, to the dry flour and crumb in the bottom of the bowl. Quickly stir again with the knife, to create large flakes, adding a little more water if necessary. You should ideally not add any more than about 8 tbsp water, or the pastry may start to toughen.

3 Feel the large flakes, and if there seems to be a good amount of moisture that is evenly distributed, pull them together in your hands and work the pastry a little to bring it together so it is homogeneous and fairly smooth. Shape this détrempe into a block about 12 x 17cm and 2–3cm thick, wrap closely in cling film and place in the fridge to relax for about 20 minutes.

4 Remove the détrempe from the fridge, unwrap and place on a floured surface, with a side end facing you. Ridge the détrempe gently, patting up and down on it and keeping the rolling pin parallel to your body, as for rough puff (see step 5, page 72).

5 Now roll with quick, short sharp rolls, gently encouraging the pastry to lengthen rather than applying too much pressure and stretching it (see step 6, page 72).

6 When the pastry is about 3 times as long as it is wide, re-check that the sides are straight and corners square, then, using a cutlery knife, dab another quarter of the cold, pliable butter over the top two thirds of the pastry, leaving a 1cm border around the edge without butter. Fold the bottom third of the pastry up over the middle third and the top third down and over the bottom and middle third, so the butter is interwoven in the layers. Turn the pastry so the folded side is to your left. This is known as a roll and fold.

7 Now commence the second roll and fold, making sure the pastry is cold to the touch and the butter is not breaking through the détrempe and becoming greasy. If it appears to be, then scatter some flour over the butter, dust it off with a pastry brush and continue. Once the pastry is 3 times as long as it is wide again, fold the pastry into three as before, this time without butter. This is known as a blind roll and fold.

8 Wrap the flaky pastry closely in cling film, making a note of how many roll and folds you have done, and place in the fridge again to relax and keep the fat cool.

9 Repeat the 2 roll and folds again, adding the third pile of butter in the third roll and fold, and the remaining butter in the fourth. Wrap closely in cling film and chill again for about 20 minutes, making sure the butter does not firm up too much.

10 Repeat a blind roll and fold (without butter), to make a total of 5 roll and folds. If the pastry is streaky, you will need a sixth, but generally flaky pastry has 5 roll and folds. Keep wrapped in the fridge until needed.

RED ONION AND GOAT'S CHEESE TARTLETS

MAKES 6

1 quantity flaky pastry
  (see left)
Extra flour, to dust
1 egg

FOR THE FILLING
3 medium red onions
30g butter
2–3 tbsp soft light brown
  sugar

75ml red wine
Few thyme sprigs
6 slices of goat's cheese, 1cm
  thick, from a crottin or log
  about 3cm in diameter
¼ bunch of thyme
About 3 tbsp olive oil
Salt and freshly ground
  black pepper

You can also make a large version of these tartlets by rolling the pastry out to a rectangle 3–4mm thick and creating a border, then pricking with a fork (as below) before covering with the topping ingredients.

1 For the filling, halve, peel and thinly slice the red onions. Heat the butter in a frying pan and add the onions. Cover, ideally with a cartouche (see page 155) and sweat the onions until softened, about 10–15 minutes. Uncover, turn up the heat to medium, stir in the sugar, to taste, and continue cooking for 10–15 minutes until the onions are golden brown. Stir in the wine and cook gently until it has mostly evaporated and the onions are a deep brown colour. This can take up to 15 minutes.

2 Finely chop enough thyme leaves to give you ¼–½ tsp and stir them into the onions. Season with salt and pepper to taste and allow to cool.

3 Roll out the chilled pastry on a lightly floured surface to a rectangle, about 3–4mm thick. Using a round pastry cutter or template about 12.5cm in diameter, cut out 6 discs of pastry as cleanly as possible. Transfer the discs to a large baking sheet, cover with cling film and chill until firm to the touch. Meanwhile, heat the oven to 200°C/gas mark 6.

4 Cut up the sides of the pastry (as shown on page 103). To create a border, use a small, sharp knife to cut a circle about 1cm in from the edge of the case; take care to cut only halfway through the pastry. Using a fork and avoiding the border, prick the pastry circle well, to stop the middle rising as it cooks.

5 Divide the caramelised onions between the tarts and spread on top of the pastry, leaving the border clear. Top with a disc of goat's cheese.

6 Lightly beat the egg with a very small pinch of salt, using a fork, then pass through a sieve into a bowl. Brush the border of each disc with the egg glaze, making sure it doesn't drip down the sides of the pastry, which could seal the layering together.

7 Using a sharp knife, lightly mark the glazed borders with patterns; these should be indentations rather than cuts. They will help control the top layers from shattering too much as they cook.

8 Bake in the oven for 20–25 minutes, or until the pastry has risen around the filling and is golden brown, the onions are hot and the cheese is starting to melt. Meanwhile, pick off ½ tsp thyme leaves.

9 If the cheese has not browned at all, a kitchen blowtorch can be used to colour it, taking care to avoid burning the pastry. Scatter the thyme leaves over the tarts and drizzle with a little olive oil, about ½ tbsp per tart. Serve hot with a lightly dressed green salad.

SALT AND PEPPER
WAFERS

MAKES about 30	
1 quantity flaky pastry (see page 80)	1 tbsp fleur de sel or flaked sea salt, plus extra to sprinkle
Extra flour, to dust	
1 tbsp mixed peppercorns (black, white, green and pink)	1 egg
	Large pinch of cayenne pepper

Mixed peppercorns, available from delicatessens and supermarkets, give these wafers a good balance of flavour. Bake the wafers in batches if oven space and baking sheets are in short supply. Keep the uncooked wafers well chilled until ready to bake. They are perfect to accompany drinks or cocktails.

1 Roll out the pastry on a lightly floured surface to a 25 x 30cm rectangle. Using a large, sharp knife, trim the edges to make a neat rectangle.

2 Finely crush the peppercorns using a pestle and mortar or with the end of a rolling pin in a small bowl. Sprinkle the crushed peppercorns and 1 tbsp salt evenly over the pastry. Fold in two, like a book, then roll out again to its original size.

3 Cut the pastry into 4 strips, across its width. Using a fork, lightly beat the egg with a very small pinch of salt and the cayenne, then pass through a sieve into a bowl.

4 Brush a band of egg wash down the centre of 3 strips and carefully place them on top of each other (as shown), with the egg wash facing upwards. Place the remaining piece on top. Press a rolling pin down along the middle of the stack of pastry to seal the bands together. Avoid pressing the edges together and keep the layers separate.

5 Cut the stack into slices at 1cm intervals (as shown). The slices will comprise 4 thin layers of pastry, joined and sealed at the centre.

6 Take one of the slices, twist it at the centre and place it on a baking sheet lined with baking parchment (as shown). Fan out each end to loosen the strips.

7 Shape the remaining slices in the same way, spacing them well apart as they will expand as they cook. Brush each with a little egg glaze, without letting it drip down the sides, then chill in the fridge for 15 minutes. Meanwhile, heat the oven to 200°C/gas mark 6.

8 Brush a little more egg glaze over each wafer and sprinkle with a little extra salt. Bake for 10–15 minutes, or until pale golden and cooked through. Remove from the oven and transfer to a wire rack to cool.

PUFF PASTRY

MAKES about 500g

250g plain flour, plus
    extra to dust
½ tsp salt

180–200g cold but pliable
    unsalted butter
100–120ml (6½–8 tbsp)
    chilled water

This is the lightest and flakiest of all the layered pastries and well worth mastering, as good homemade puff pastry is far superior to even the best bought puff pastries. Some butter is added to the détrempe, or base dough, but most of it is incorporated by rolling a block of cool but flexible butter into the dough with 6 roll and folds. Puff pastry should rise to 3 times its height when baked.

1 Sift the flour and salt into a medium bowl. Cut a 30g piece from the butter, then cut this into small cubes and add to the flour and salt. Rub into the flour with your fingertips until it resembles fine breadcrumbs (see step 3, page 12). Add 100ml chilled water and, using a cutlery knife, mix everything together quickly and efficiently for about 15–20 seconds, turning the bowl as you stir.

2 The crumb and water will form large flakes. Drag the large flakes to the side of the bowl and add more water, ½ tbsp at a time, to the dry crumb in the bottom of the bowl. Stir again quickly to create large flakes and add a little more water if necessary. You should ideally not add more than about 8 tbsp water, or the pastry may start to toughen.

3 Feel the large flakes, and if there seems to be a good amount of moisture within them and the water is evenly distributed, pull the large flakes together in your hands and work the pastry a little to bring the détrempe together into a homogeneous pastry that is fairly smooth and a uniform colour. Shape into a block about 12 x 17cm and 2–3cm thick, wrap closely in cling film and place in the fridge for 20 minutes.

4 Unwrap the puff pastry and place on a floured surface, with a short end facing you. Ridge gently, patting up and down on the pastry, keeping the rolling pin parallel to you. Try to keep the sides straight and the corners of the pastry square, using a palette knife or your hands, but keep hand contact to a minimum to prevent the pastry from warming up. Keep ridging as much as possible before you roll, then roll with quick, short, sharp rolls, gently encouraging the pastry to lengthen rather than applying too much pressure and stretching it. When the pastry is about twice as long as it is wide, re-check the sides are straight and corners square.

5 Place the remaining butter between 2 sheets of greaseproof paper. Bash with a rolling pin to flatten, then shape into a rectangle half the size of the rolled détrempe. If the butter gets too big, fold it. At this stage it should still be cold and, if it folds without breaking, it is pliable enough. Neaten it quickly to a rectangle and check it for size.

6 Place the butter on the bottom half of the détrempe, press the border lightly to flatten it, then bring the edges of the détrempe up the sides of the butter and press them over the edge of the butter. Bring the top half down over the exposed butter. Press the edges down against the sides of the butter, ensuring a good seal; the butter must not be able to escape.

7 With the folded side away from you, ridge and then roll the pastry to 3 times as long as it is wide, keeping the sides straight and the corners square. Avoid creating thick ends at the top and bottom; roll back a little if necessary and avoid rolling over the top and bottom edge as you will stretch the top layer and create uneven layers, which will result in uneven rising.

(Technique continued overleaf)

1 Mixing the ingredients together quickly, using a cutlery knife.

2 Feeling the flakes to see if any more water is needed.

3 Pulling the large flakes together in your hands to start to bring the dough together.

4 Gently ridging the rested détrempe with the rolling pin.

(Continued overleaf)

5 Flattening the butter between 2 sheets of greaseproof paper.

6 Bringing the edges of the détrempe up the sides of the butter.

7 Rolling the butter-enclosed détrempe out until it is 3 times as long as it is wide.

8 Folding the bottom third of the pastry up over the middle third, before folding the top down.

9 After folding the top third down, the pastry is turned 90° so the fold is at the left.

8 Fold the bottom third of the pastry over the middle third, then the top third down over the bottom and middle third.

9 Now turn the pastry 90° so the fold is at your left. This completes the first roll and fold.

10 Now repeat the roll and fold, making sure the pastry is always cold to the touch and the butter is not breaking through the détrempe and becoming greasy. If it is, then scatter some flour over the butter, dust it off with a pastry brush and continue. When making puff, all the roll and folds are 'blind', as all the butter has already been incorporated. Wrap closely, making a note of how many roll and folds you have done, and place in the fridge again to relax and keep the butter cool and firm, for about 20 minutes. The butter must be cool but pliable, so don't let it firm up too much in the fridge.

11 Repeat the 2 roll and folds again twice, covering the pastry closely and chilling for about 20 minutes after each 2 roll and folds, and making a note of how many roll and folds you have done. Once the pastry has had 6 roll and folds, it can be kept in the fridge until needed. If very streaky, you may need to do one more roll and fold.

A note on butter content...

This recipe gives a range of butter quantity. If making puff for the first time, use the smaller amount. When you are confident with the method and the pastry works for you, increase the amount of butter for a richer flavour.

Making puff pastry in advance...

If making puff pastry either the day before use or for freezing, don't complete the last roll and fold. Wrap the pastry closely in cling film, mark the number of roll and folds on the cling film and chill or freeze. Defrost frozen pastry in the fridge over 24 hours; it must be kept chilled when defrosting or the butter within the layers may melt.

If you have chilled the pastry for more than 2–3 hours, leave it at room temperature for 5 minutes before rolling out, to allow it to soften very slightly. When ready to use, perform the last roll and fold which will help to 'refresh' the pastry and release the layers.

A note on using ready-made puff pastry...

Bought puff pastry will generally rise higher and more evenly than homemade puff pastry so if you choose to use it, for some recipes it may need to be rolled out a little thinner.

CHICKEN AND WILD MUSHROOM PIE

SERVES 4

FOR THE CHICKEN AND POACHING LIQUOR
1 chicken, about 1.3kg
1 onion
1 carrot
1 celery stick
2 parsley sprigs
6 black peppercorns
2 bay leaves
Salt and freshly ground
    black pepper

FOR THE PIE
250g puff pastry (see page
    84, or use ready-made)
1 small onion
150g wild mushrooms, such
    as chanterelles or porcini
Small handful of chives
40g butter
30g plain flour
50ml white wine or Marsala
5 tbsp crème fraîche
1 egg, to glaze

You will need a 1–1.2 litre pie dish.

1 Put the chicken into a large pan, cover with cold water and slowly bring to the boil over a medium to low heat. Halve, peel and slice the onion, peel and slice the carrot, de-string and slice the celery. Add them to the pan with the parsley, peppercorns, bay leaves and some salt. As the water comes to the boil, turn the heat down and cover with a tight-fitting lid. Poach the chicken gently for 1–1¼ hours; it is cooked when the legs feel loose and the juices run clear when a skewer is inserted into the thickest part of the thigh.

2 While the chicken is poaching, roll out the chilled pastry on a floured surface until 3–4mm thick and about 5cm larger than the pie dish all round. Cut strips from the edge that together will line the lip of the pie dish. Put all the pastry on a baking sheet, cover and chill.

3 Halve, peel and finely dice the onion. Wipe the mushrooms clean, trimming if necessary, and halve or quarter, depending on size. Finely chop enough chives to give you 1 tbsp.

4 When the chicken is cooked, let it cool a little in the liquor, then remove it and allow to cool completely. Strain the liquor, discarding the vegetables and herbs, and pour it back into the rinsed out saucepan. Skim off the fat, then reduce to 350–400ml to concentrate the flavour. Set aside for the sauce. Once cold, remove any skin, gristle and bone from the chicken, then break into large bite-sized pieces and set aside.

5 To make the sauce, melt the butter in a pan over a low heat. Add the onion and sweat for 8–10 minutes, or until soft and transparent. Increase the heat, add the mushrooms and sauté for 5–7 minutes. Lower the heat, add the flour and cook for 3–4 minutes. Remove from the heat and gradually stir in the wine, then about half of the reduced liquor. Return the pan to the heat and stir in the remaining liquor in generous additions. Bring to the boil, stirring, then lower the heat and simmer for 2 minutes. Stir in the chives and crème fraîche, taste and season with salt and pepper. Transfer to a bowl and allow to cool.

6 Lightly beat the egg with a pinch of salt, then sieve it. Add the chicken to the cold sauce and turn the pieces to coat evenly. Spoon the filling into the pie dish, making sure there is enough filling to support the pastry lid. If not, use a pie funnel (see page 36). Press the pastry strips onto the rim of the dish and brush with a little beaten egg. Carefully position the pastry lid on top and press the edges gently to join. Trim off the excess.

7 Cut out leaves from the pastry trimmings. Knock up the pastry with the back of a knife and scallop the edges (as shown on page 103). Make a hole in the centre of the lid to allow steam to escape and arrange the leaves on top of the pie. Brush the pastry with beaten egg. Stand the dish on a baking sheet and chill for 15–20 minutes. Heat the oven to 200°C/gas mark 6.

8 Brush the pie again with egg. Bake in the top of the oven for 25–30 minutes, or until the pastry is golden and the filling is hot.

FILLET OF BEEF EN CROÛTE

SERVES 6–8

1 piece of fillet of beef, from
    the thick end, about 1.3kg
Dash of Worcestershire sauce
    (optional)
1 tbsp olive oil
350g puff pastry (see page
    84, or use ready-made)
100g chestnut mushrooms

1 garlic clove
¼ bunch of thyme
30g butter
100g good quality smooth
    chicken liver pâté
1 egg, to glaze
Salt and freshly ground
    black pepper

1 Heat the oven to 230°C/gas mark 8.

2 Trim the fillet and season well with salt, pepper and Worcestershire sauce, if using. Tie with string at 2–3cm intervals to help hold its shape. Heat the olive oil in a roasting tin over a medium to high heat and brown the meat evenly on all sides.

3 Transfer the meat to the oven and roast for 15 minutes. This will give you rare beef once the fillet is baked within the pastry; for medium allow a further 10 minutes at this early stage; for well done meat allow a further 15 minutes. Remove the fillet from the roasting tin, leave to cool and remove all the string.

4 Roll out one third of the pastry on a floured board until it is a little more than the length and width of the fillet. Place on a baking sheet, prick all over with a fork and bake for 20 minutes, or until golden. Transfer to a wire rack and leave to cool.

5 Wipe and finely chop the mushrooms, peel and crush the garlic; finely chop enough thyme leaves to give 1 tsp. Heat the butter in a frying pan over a medium to high heat and fry the mushrooms quickly to release and evaporate their liquid. Add the garlic and thyme and cook for 1 minute; the mixture should be dry. Allow to cool completely.

6 Mix the mushrooms with the pâté, check the seasoning, then spread over the cooled fillet of beef and place it on the cooked pastry sheet. Cut away any pastry not covered by the fillet.

7 Roll out the remaining pastry on a floured board until large enough to cover the fillet easily. Lay it gently over the fillet. Lightly press the pastry to the fillet and seal the corners. Cut off any excess pastry at the corners; reserve the trimmings.

8 With a palette knife, lift the cooked pastry base and tuck the uncooked pastry edge neatly underneath it. Repeat with the other 3 sides. The pastry trimmings can be used to cut strips or leaves to decorate the top. If the pastry is very soft, loosely cover it with cling film and chill the parcel in the fridge for 15 minutes before baking (see note on preparing ahead).

9 Lightly beat the egg with a small pinch of salt, then pass through a sieve. Brush the pastry with the beaten egg, stick any decorations on the pastry, then brush again with egg.

10 Bake in the middle of the oven for 20–30 minutes, or until the pastry is dark brown and shiny. Remove and leave to rest for 15–20 minutes before carving.

A note on preparing ahead...

✳ You can prepare this in advance up to the end of stage 8, prior to glazing. Loosely cover with cling film and place in the fridge until ready to cook.

Enveloping the beef in crêpes...

✳ Traditionally, crêpes are wrapped around the beef fillet and pâté before encasing in pastry to help to keep the pastry crisp. If you do this, wrap in a single layer of crêpes, trimming as necessary to ensure minimal overlap.

ARTICHOKE AND GREEN OLIVE PITHIVIER

SERVES 6

1 quantity puff pastry
   (see page 84, or use
   500g ready-made)
Extra flour, to dust
1 egg

FOR THE FILLING
400g tin artichoke hearts
   in brine, drained
5 shallots

1 garlic clove
¼ bunch of thyme
¼ bunch of sage
75g green olives
30g butter
30ml vermouth
75ml double cream
Salt and freshly ground
   black pepper

Conveniently, this delicious pie can be prepared ahead and refrigerated until ready to bake.

1 For the filling, cut the artichokes into pieces. Halve, peel and finely dice the shallots, and peel and crush the garlic. Finely chop enough thyme and sage to give you ½–1 tsp of each. Stone and halve the olives.

2 Melt the butter in a medium saucepan and sweat the shallots over a low heat until starting to turn soft and translucent. Add the artichokes, thyme and sage and cook gently until the shallots are very soft. Add the garlic and cook for 1 minute, then add the vermouth and reduce by half. Add the cream and reduce to a light coating consistency, stirring occasionally to prevent the mixture burning on the bottom of the pan.

3 Transfer the mixture to a bowl to cool, add the olives and season with salt and pepper to taste.

4 Cut the chilled pastry into 2 pieces, one slightly bigger than the other. On a lightly floured surface, roll out the smaller piece to a large square about 3mm thick. Using a large, sharp knife, cut out a disc of pastry, about 24cm in diameter, using a saucepan lid to cut round and making as few cuts as possible to avoid dragging through the pastry as you cut. Place the pastry disc on a baking sheet and chill in the fridge.

5 Roll out the larger piece of pastry to a slightly larger square, and cut out a circle about 26cm in diameter, and ideally slightly thicker than 3mm, in the same way as the smaller disc. Place on a second baking sheet and chill until needed.

6 Remove the first pastry disc from the fridge and spoon the filling onto the pastry, leaving a 2.5cm clear border around the edge. Flatten the filling a little into a disc 2.5–3cm thick. Beat the egg lightly using a fork and pass through a sieve into a small bowl.

7 Using a pastry brush, brush the border with beaten egg and carefully place the larger pastry disc over the filling, smoothing it out from the middle of the filling to remove any air bubbles. Press the edges together firmly to seal.

8 Cut around the top layer of pastry using the bottom layer as a guide, then 'cut up' the sides of the pastry (as shown on page 103) and scallop the edges, by placing 2 fingers lightly on the pastry rim and drawing the back of a cutlery knife between your fingers and upwards (as shown on page 103).

9 Glaze the pastry with the beaten egg, then score the top of the pastry from the centre to the edges, curving the scoring like the petals of a flower, without cutting right through the pastry to the filling. Chill for 20 minutes until firm to the touch. Meanwhile, heat the oven to 220°C/gas mark 7.

10 Glaze the top again with egg, making sure the glaze does not drip down the scalloped edges. Bake for 35–45 minutes until the pastry has risen, is a deep golden colour and firm to the touch at the sides.

11 Remove from the oven, transfer to a wire rack to cool and serve either warm or at room temperature, with a leafy salad.

PORK AND FENNEL SAUSAGE ROLLS

MAKES 10 large or 20 small rolls

1 quantity puff pastry
   (see page 84, or use
   500g ready-made)
Extra flour, to dust
1 egg
1 tsp fennel seeds

FOR THE FILLING
1 onion
1 celery stick
2 tbsp olive oil
2 garlic cloves
2 tbsp fennel seeds
1kg pork mince
Salt and freshly ground
   black pepper

If you make small cocktail-sized sausage rolls, they can be frozen raw and then cooked directly from the freezer, adding 5–10 minutes to the cooking time.

1 For the filling, halve, peel and very finely dice the onion and de-string and very finely dice the celery. Heat the olive oil in a small saucepan, add the onion and celery, cover and sweat over a low heat until soft and translucent. Meanwhile, peel and crush the garlic and crush the fennel seeds using a pestle and mortar.

2 When the onion and celery are very soft, add the garlic and cook for 1 minute, then add the crushed fennel seeds and cook for a further 1 minute. Transfer the mixture to a bowl and allow to cool.

3 Once cool, add the pork mince and mix thoroughly. Season with salt and pepper. To check the seasoning, heat a frying pan over a medium heat and fry 1 tbsp of the mixture in a splash of oil until cooked. Taste and adjust the seasoning of the main mixture as necessary.

4 Roll out the chilled pastry on a lightly floured surface to a large rectangle, 30 x 34cm and about 3mm thick. Trim off the edges using a large knife, then cut the rectangle in half, each piece measuring 30 x 17cm.

5 Take about half the filling and shape it between the palms of your hands into a sausage shape, about 2–3cm in diameter. Lay it along the length of the pastry. Lightly dampening your hands with water before shaping will help prevent the filling from sticking to your hands.

6 Lightly beat the egg with a very small pinch of salt, using a fork, then pass through a sieve into a bowl. Brush a little down one long side of the pastry. Roll the pastry closely over the filling and seal over the egg washed side, ensuring a good seal.

7 Repeat with the remaining pastry and filling, then cut into 6cm lengths, or shorter pieces for smaller sausage rolls. Place on a baking tray, sealed sides down and glaze with beaten egg. Chill in the fridge for 20–30 minutes. Meanwhile, heat the oven to 190°C/gas mark 5.

8 When the pastry is firm to the touch, brush each sausage roll with the beaten egg again, scatter with fennel seeds, then bake in the top of the oven for about 30 minutes until the pastry is a deep golden colour. Check the filling is cooked by inserting a skewer into the middle of a sausage roll. Leave it for 10 seconds, then remove it and check the heat of the skewer against the inside of your wrist; it should be hot. If not, return to the oven for a further 5–10 minutes. If they are browning too much, place them on a lower shelf.

9 Remove the sausage rolls from the oven and leave to cool a little before serving.

Variation

✳ Pork and herb sausage rolls Omit the fennel seeds and add 2 tbsp very finely chopped mixed herbs, such as parsley, sage, thyme and chives, to the filling.

PALMIERS

MAKES about 20

About 250g puff pastry
  trimmings and leftovers
  (see below)

100g caster sugar

1 Lay the puff pastry trimming pieces flat on top of each other (rather than squidge them together), folding them if necessary.

2 Use about half of the caster sugar to dust the work surface and roll the pastry out into a rectangle 5mm thick. Sprinkle well with 2–3 tbsp caster sugar. Roll the long ends of the pastry into the middle, where they will meet (as shown).

3 Cut the roll across into 1cm wide slices. Lay the slices flat on a damp baking sheet, set well apart, and flatten well using a rolling pin or your fingers.

4 Cover with cling film and chill in the fridge for 15 minutes until firm. Meanwhile, heat the oven to 200°C/gas mark 6.

5 Sprinkle with a little more caster sugar and bake in the oven for 10 minutes, or until pale golden and cooked through, with the underside caramelised. Turn them over and bake for a further 10 minutes. Remove from the oven, transfer to a wire rack and leave to cool.

Note

✽ These palmiers are an excellent way of using up trimmings and off-cuts from other recipes. When saving the trimmings, don't roll them into a ball, or it will spoil the carefully created layering in the pastry.

PORTUGUESE CUSTARD TARTS

MAKES 18

1 quantity puff pastry
(see page 84)
Extra flour, to dust

FOR THE FILLING
6 egg yolks
4 tbsp cornflour
250g caster sugar
350ml milk
550ml double cream
3 tsp vanilla extract
Icing sugar, to dust

You will need two 9-hole (or 12-hole) muffin tins.

1 Roll out the chilled pastry on a lightly floured surface to a 2–3mm thickness. Use a 9cm pastry cutter to stamp out 18 circles. (You may need to layer up and re-roll the trimmings to get 18.) Press each circle into a muffin tin, ensuring that they are lightly pressed right into the bottom corners. Cover with cling film and refrigerate for at least 30 minutes, or until completely firm.

2 Meanwhile, to make the custard, put the egg yolks, cornflour and sugar in a large bowl and mix well to combine. Gradually add the milk and then the cream, whisking well to stir out any lumps after each addition. When all the milk and cream have been added and the mixture is smooth, transfer to a saucepan and cook over a low heat, stirring slowly and constantly until it starts to steam and thickens considerably to the consistency of Greek yoghurt. This may take up to 20 minutes. To avoid the yolks curdling, it is important that the mixture doesn't boil.

3 Immediately transfer the thickened custard to a large bowl and add the vanilla extract. Taste and adjust as necessary, adding a little more sugar or vanilla if needed. Lay a sheet of cling film directly onto the surface of the mixture, to prevent a skin from forming. Allow to cool, then chill in the fridge.

4 Heat the oven to 190°C/gas mark 5 and place a large baking sheet in the top third of the oven to heat up.

5 Take the muffin tins out of the fridge and divide the custard evenly between the pastry cases. Place on the hot baking sheet in the oven and bake for 20–25 minutes until the pastry is risen, golden and cooked through and the custard is set. It is normal for the custard to have dark patches.

6 Take the tarts out of the oven and leave to cool in the tins for 5–10 minutes, then gently remove from the tins and transfer to a wire rack to cool completely. Lightly dust with icing sugar and serve.

INDIVIDUAL TARTE AUX POMMES

MAKES 4

FOR THE APPLE PURÉE
750g (3 medium)
  Bramley apples
3 tbsp water
40g caster sugar
1 tbsp Calvados
1 orange

FOR THE TARTS
½ quantity puff pastry
  (see page 84)
Extra flour, to dust
2 dessert apples
1 egg
Caster sugar, to sprinkle
1 quantity apricot glaze
  (see page 153)

These appealing individual tarts are slightly more robust and easier to handle than the elegant galettes found in French patisseries. They are perfect served as an autumnal pudding.

1 To make the purée, peel and core the apples, cut into thin slices and put into a medium saucepan with the water, sugar and Calvados. Finely grate the zest from half of the orange and add to the pan.

2 Cover and cook over a very gentle heat until the apples have softened and lost their shape. Stir to break them up, remove the lid and continue to cook until completely smooth and very thick. Taste and add more sugar if necessary. Remove from the heat and allow to cool, spreading the apple purée out on a cold plate to cool it down faster if necessary.

3 Roll out the chilled pastry on a lightly floured surface to a 3mm thickness and, using a 12.5cm plain pastry cutter, stamp out 4 discs. It is easier to roll the pastry into an oblong, just wider than the cutter, in order to cut the 4 discs out in a row.

4 Place the pastry discs on a baking tray and, using a sharp knife, trace an inner circle about 1cm from the edge of each pastry disc without cutting all the way through the pastry. Cover with cling film and chill in the fridge. Meanwhile, heat the oven to 200°C/gas mark 6.

5 Peel, core and finely slice the dessert apples. Using a fork, lightly beat the egg and pass through a sieve into a small bowl.

6 Spoon about 1 tbsp of the cooled apple purée into the centre of each pastry circle and spread it out evenly over the pastry, stopping at the border to leave it clear. Arrange the apple slices in concentric circles over the top of the purée, overlapping like flower petals within the border, or tightly overlap the slices in a spiral shape. Brush the border of each pastry disc with a little beaten egg, trying not to drip it down the edge.

7 Sprinkle each tart with a light dusting of caster sugar and bake in the top third of the oven for 20 minutes, or until the pastry is brown and risen and the apples are starting to brown on their edges. Warm the apricot glaze just before the tarts will be cooked.

8 Remove from the oven and brush the tarts generously with the warm apricot glaze. Serve warm or cold with cream, crème fraîche, crème anglaise or ice cream.

MAPLE PECAN JALOUSIE

SERVES 6

1 quantity puff pastry
  (see page 84)
Extra flour, to dust
1 egg

FOR THE FILLING
80g pecan nuts
50g soft dark brown sugar
200ml maple syrup
2 drops of vanilla extract
1 egg
Salt

'Jalousie' is French for shutters, which the pastry is cut to resemble. This works fantastically well for all manner of fillings, as the 'shutters' let out all the steam and reveal some of the delicious filling within.

1 Roll out the chilled pastry on a lightly floured surface to a 30cm square, 3mm thick. Cut in two, so that one rectangle is slightly wider than the other.

2 Lightly roll out the larger rectangle so that it is also a little longer than the smaller one, and trim all the edges. Place the rectangles on 2 separate baking sheets lined with baking parchment, cover with cling film and chill in the fridge for 20 minutes. Meanwhile, heat the oven to 200°C/gas mark 6.

3 Beat the egg using a fork and pass through a sieve into a small bowl. Take the smaller chilled pastry rectangle from the fridge, prick it all over with a fork, then brush with some of the beaten egg (as shown). Bake in the top third of the oven for 15 minutes, until starting to take on colour but not fully cooked through. Remove from the oven and set aside.

4 Take the other pastry rectangle from the fridge, lightly dust with flour and gently fold it over in half lengthways, making sure the sides don't stick together. Using a sharp knife, cut parallel lines about 1cm apart through the folded side of the pastry, at right angles to the edges, stopping 1.5cm from the open edge (as shown). Unfold the pastry and chill in the fridge until ready to use.

5 To make the filling, coarsely chop the pecans and place in a bowl. Add the sugar, 60ml of the maple syrup, the vanilla extract and a pinch of salt. Beat the egg with a fork, add to the nut mixture and stir well to combine.

6 To assemble the jalousie, brush a 1.5cm border of beaten egg all the way around the edge of the cooked base. Spoon the pecan mixture evenly onto the pastry, leaving the border clear. Place the larger, jalousie-pattern pastry over the pecan mixture, line up the borders on the top and bottom pastries and lightly press to seal together. If necessary, tuck the upper edges under the bottom layer of pastry or simply trim the edges, using a large chef's knife.

7 Brush the top of the pastry with the remaining beaten egg, making sure the egg doesn't seep into the slits in the pastry. Bake in the top third of the oven for 25–30 minutes until the pastry is cooked through and golden.

8 Remove the jalousie from the oven and, while still hot, pour over the remaining maple syrup and allow to soak in through the gaps in the 'shutters'. Cut into slices and serve warm with a generous scoop of vanilla ice cream.

RHUBARB AND CUSTARD JALOUSIE

SERVES 6

1 quantity puff pastry
(see page 84)
Extra flour, to dust
1 egg white
Caster sugar, to sprinkle

FOR THE FILLING
750g pink (forced) rhubarb
2 tbsp caster sugar
3 tbsp rhubarb jam, sieved
1½ tbsp rhubarb and
strawberry cordial
½ quantity crème pâtissière,
well chilled (see page 152)

This classic flavour combination is best when rhubarb is at its delicate pinkest. If you can't find rhubarb jam, rhubarb compote or strawberry jam also work well. If you cannot find rhubarb and strawberry cordial, you can use any other red fruit or floral cordial, such as raspberry or elderflower.

1 Divide the chilled pastry equally in two. Roll out on a lightly floured surface into 2 thin rectangles, one about 2.5cm bigger all round than the other, with the smaller one about 13 x 20cm and the larger 18 x 25cm. Trim the edges.

2 Place the smaller rectangle on a baking sheet lined with baking parchment, prick all over with a fork and chill until firm, about 20 minutes. Meanwhile, heat the oven to 200°C/gas mark 6.

3 Dust the other rectangle lightly with flour and gently fold it over in half lengthways, making sure the sides don't stick together. Using a sharp knife, cut parallel lines about 1cm apart through the folded side of the pastry, at right angles to the edges, stopping 2.5cm from the open edge (as shown on page 99). Unfold the pastry and refrigerate until ready to use.

4 For the filling, trim the rhubarb stalks and cut into batons, about 7cm long. Wash and dry well on kitchen paper. Place on a lipped baking sheet lined with non-stick baking parchment so that the pieces are just touching and sprinkle over the sugar. Bake in the middle of the oven for 10–15 minutes, or until just

tender when pierced with the tip of a knife. It should be soft and cooked through but still holding its shape. Using a palette knife, transfer the rhubarb to a large plate, taking care not to break up the pieces and pour on any cooking juices over the rhubarb. Leave to cool, then chill.

5 Bake the smaller rectangle of pastry in the top third of the oven for 20–25 minutes, or until golden brown and cooked through. Spread the rhubarb jam over the warm pastry, using the back of a tablespoon or a palette knife, and return to the oven for 1–2 minutes to set the jam (this creates a seal to keep the pastry crisp when filled). Transfer to a wire rack to cool.

6 Meanwhile, pour the cordial over the rhubarb and leave to stand at room temperature for about 5 minutes.

7 To assemble the jalousie, spread the chilled crème pâtissière over the cooked, cooled pastry base, leaving a 1cm border. Place the rhubarb on top, laying the batons out evenly, and pour over any juices left on the plate.

8 Place the jalousie-pattern pastry on top and tuck the edges underneath the base. Using a fork, beat the egg white until frothy and brush over the top, taking care not to seal the cuts together. Sprinkle generously with caster sugar.

9 Bake for 20–25 minutes until risen and well browned, and the top layer of pastry is cooked through. Transfer to a wire rack to cool and serve at room temperature or slightly chilled.

MILLEFEUILLE OF CHERRIES AND ALMOND CREAM

MAKES 4

1 quantity puff pastry
  (see page 84)
Extra flour, to dust
½ quantity almond cream
  (see page 50)

FOR THE CHERRIES
400g cherries
20g unsalted butter
15g soft light brown sugar
1 tsp Kirsch

FOR THE MINT OIL
Small bunch of mint
150ml sunflower oil

FOR THE SABAYON
2 egg yolks
3 tbsp caster sugar
25ml Champagne
25ml double cream

TO FINISH
Icing sugar, to dust

This millefeuille is a real show-stopper. If you don't have time to make the sabayon and mint oil, these pastries can be served simply with a dusting of icing sugar. Any seasonal fruit can be substituted for the cherries: raspberries or small strawberries can be used fresh without cooking in the sugar and butter, and caramelised poached pears work well in the same way.

1 Heat the oven to 200°C/gas mark 6.

2 Roll out the chilled puff pastry on a lightly floured surface to a large rectangle, 2mm thick. Trim the edges and transfer to a baking tray. Prick the pastry all over with a fork, then place another baking tray on top of the pastry. You might need to cut the pastry in half and cook half at a time if it is too big.

3 Bake in the oven for 20–30 minutes until cooked through and deep golden. Carefully remove the top baking tray and let the pastry cool before cutting into 12 rectangles, each 5 x 7.5cm.

4 Stone the cherries and put with the butter, sugar and Kirsch in a small saucepan over a low heat. Let the butter and sugar melt to a sauce and warm the cherries, then take off the heat.

5 Pick the leaves from the mint and blanch in boiling water for a few seconds, then refresh in cold water. Drain and place with the oil in a blender. Blend well to break down the mint, leave to infuse for 30 minutes, then strain through a muslin-lined sieve.

6 For the sabayon, put the egg yolks, sugar and half the Champagne in a heatproof bowl big enough to sit over a saucepan of simmering water. Set the bowl over the pan, making sure the base is not in direct contact with the water.

7 Using a hand-held electric whisk, whisk the mixture for up to 10 minutes until it has increased in volume and is light and mousse-like. Remove the bowl from the heat and continue to whisk until the mixture is cool (this will take several minutes).

8 Meanwhile, in a separate bowl, whip the cream to soft peaks, then fold it into the sabayon with the remaining Champagne. Chill until ready for use (but for no longer than 2 hours).

9 To assemble the dish, place the almond cream in a piping bag fitted with a 5mm plain nozzle and pipe the cream in neat lines on top of 8 pastry rectangles, ensuring all the pastry is covered.

10 Cover the 8 almond cream topped pastries with a layer of cherries. Carefully stack these cherry topped pastries in pairs, then top each with a final pastry rectangle to create 4 individual millefeuille. Dust the tops with icing sugar.

11 Carefully transfer to individual plates. Spoon any remaining cherries and sauce to the side of each millefeuille, then spoon 1–2 tbsp sabayon over the cherries. Drizzle a few drops of the mint oil around each before serving.

RED BERRY JAMBOREE

SERVES 6–8

½ quantity puff pastry
  (see page 84)
Extra flour, to dust
1 egg
Caster sugar, to sprinkle
Salt

FOR THE GANACHE
150g good quality white
  chocolate
150ml double cream
Seeds from ½ vanilla pod

FOR THE BERRY PURÉE
125g raspberries
2 tbsp Framboise syrup
Finely grated zest of ½ lemon

FOR THE TOPPING
125g small strawberries
125g raspberries
125g blackberries
85g redcurrants
½ quantity redcurrant glaze
  (see page 153)

A wonderfully extravagant summer fruit and white chocolate tart for high days and holidays.

1 Roll out the chilled pastry on a lightly floured surface to a 4mm thickness. Using a large, sharp knife, cut out a 22cm circle using a plate as a template. Place the pastry on a baking sheet, cover with cling film and chill in the fridge for at least 20 minutes, or until firm. Heat the oven to 200°C/gas mark 6.

2 'Cut up' the sides of the pastry (as shown). To create a border, use a small, very sharp knife to cut about halfway through the pastry about 2.5cm in from the edge. Prick the inner circle of the pastry all over, to prevent it from rising as it cooks and scallop the pastry edge (as shown).

3 Using a fork, lightly beat the egg with a very small pinch of salt, then pass through a sieve into a bowl. Brush the pastry all over with beaten egg, avoiding dripping any down the sides.

4 Bake in the top third of the oven for about 15–20 minutes until golden with a risen border. Remove from the oven and lightly brush the scalloped edge with beaten egg. Sprinkle with a little caster sugar, then carefully remove the pastry from the baking sheet and slide it directly onto the oven shelf, for the base to cook through and to lightly caramelise the sugar, about 5 minutes. If the middle of the pastry case has risen, gently press it down while still warm using the back of a tablespoon. Carefully transfer to a wire rack to cool.

5 Meanwhile, to make the ganache, chop the chocolate into small pieces and place in a heatproof bowl. Pour the cream into a small saucepan, add the vanilla seeds and bring to a simmer over a medium heat. Pour the hot cream over the chocolate and stir gently until the chocolate has melted and the mixture is well combined. Remove from the heat and leave to cool until it begins to thicken a little around the edges, then beat gently with a balloon whisk until thickened a little. Do not beat it too vigorously, or it may curdle. Keep cool but do not refrigerate.

6 To make the purée, put the raspberries, Framboise syrup and lemon zest in a small saucepan. Bring to the boil over a medium heat and cook rapidly until reduced to a thick purée. Pass through a sieve into a bowl, using a plastic spatula to make sure all the fruit pulp is pressed off the seeds. When cool, cover with cling film and chill in the fridge.

7 To assemble the tart, spread the ganache carefully over the centre of the cooled pastry, leaving the border clean. Chill in the fridge for 10 minutes. Drizzle the raspberry purée on top of the chilled ganache and, using the back of a teaspoon, spread it out to the border. Don't worry if it looks a little untidy.

8 Hull the strawberries and arrange them with the other berries on top of the tart, making sure the different varieties are evenly distributed. Glaze the fruit with the warmed redcurrant glaze, avoiding the border. Place in the fridge to set for 30 minutes before serving.

4

STRUDEL PASTRY

Although no doubt many purist Middle Eastern and Austrian cooks would strongly disagree, strudel and filo pastries are incredibly similar and can be used interchangeably; indeed historically strudel pastry, a classic of Austrian patisserie, was derived from the Middle Eastern filo.

Here we show how to make strudel pastry by hand, and although filo is widely available and can be used in place of homemade strudel in all of the recipes in this chapter, we think homemade is more delicious and worth the effort of making. We do admit that it is less uniform than bought filo, but this can be an endearing characteristic.

TECHNIQUE
STRUDEL PASTRY

MAKES about 500g

300g plain flour,
   plus extra to dust
Pinch of salt

1 egg
150ml water
1 tsp light olive oil

Strudel pastry is a very thin pastry that is traditionally stretched by hand. It is used to wrap around fillings in several layers and cooks to a crisp texture.

1 Sift the flour and salt into a medium bowl. Beat the egg in a small bowl, then add the water and oil. Using a cutlery knife, mix the egg liquid into the flour until it forms large flakes.

2 Feel the flakes and, if they feel dry, add about 1 tbsp more water at a time, until you feel the pastry come together into a soft, not sticky dough.

3 Lift the dough up in one hand and, with a flick of the wrist, slap the dough onto the work surface. If the dough is very sticky, lightly flour the work surface. Continue kneading in this way until the dough becomes very elastic, no longer sticks to your fingers and is smooth, about 8–10 minutes. This kneading technique is to develop the gluten, which will allow you to stretch the dough into a very thin sheet.

4 You should be able to stretch it out between your hands to 75–100cm. Wrap the dough well in cling film and leave to rest at room temperature for at least 15–20 minutes, to allow the gluten to relax and make it easier to stretch.

5 After resting the dough is now ready for rolling and stretching. Line one side of your work surface with a tea towel and liberally sprinkle with flour. On a clear part of the work surface, roll the dough out to a large circle, about 30cm in diameter.

6 Place your hand underneath the dough, palm uppermost and, from the centre of the circle, gently tug at the dough with your fingertips encouraging it to stretch. Don't be too forceful, or it will tear.

7 Stretch and pull, then turn the dough, to ensure an even stretching. Keep doing this until the dough becomes very thin.

8 The strudel pastry is ready when it is almost paper thin; you should be able to see through it. Trim off the thicker edges. It will dry out very quickly and become brittle, so either use immediately, brush with melted butter or cover with cling film.

A note on stretching the dough...

Stretching the dough is much easier with two people, but possible to do on your own. If a few holes appear, don't worry; once the pastry is filled and rolled the holes will disappear, and even if there are some holes on the top of the strudel the pastry around the edges will cook to a lovely crispness.

A note on using ready-made filo...

When using bought filo pastry, remove and work with one piece at a time, keeping the rest covered with a slightly damp cloth or well wrapped in cling film. It dries out quickly when exposed to the air and becomes impossible to roll or shape.

In the recipes we have given only an approximate number of sheets required when using bought filo pastry, as the dimensions of sheets vary greatly. However, if you buy a 250g pack you will have enough for the recipe and some left over. It is always a good idea to have a few sheets too many, in case any become too brittle to use.

1 Adding the egg liquid to the flour and mixing it in, using a cutlery knife.

2 Feeling the flakes of strudel pastry to check whether more water needs to be added.

3 Slapping the dough onto the work surface to knead it.

4 Stretching the dough out to check its elasticity.

(Continued overleaf)

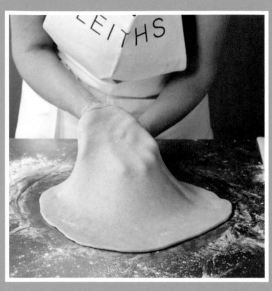

5 Rolling the strudel dough out to a large circle, about 30cm in diameter.

6 Placing one hand under the dough and gently tugging it with your fingertips to stretch it carefully, without tearing.

7 Turning the dough with your hands, to ensure even stretching.

8 Checking that the dough is sufficiently stretched. It should be possible to see through it.

MOROCCAN SPINACH AND CHICKPEA STRUDEL

SERVES 4–6	

85g butter
1 quantity strudel pastry
   (see page 106) or 6–8
   sheets of bought filo
Extra flour, to dust

FOR THE FILLING
2 red onions
1 red pepper
80g dried apricots
1 garlic clove
400g tin chickpeas
200g baby spinach leaves

Large handful of coriander
1 tbsp olive oil
1 tsp tomato purée
1 tsp harissa paste
1 tsp coriander seeds
1 tsp cumin seeds
½ tsp crushed dried chillies
½ tsp smoked paprika
¼ tsp ground cinnamon
400g tin chopped tomatoes
100g flaked almonds
Salt and freshly ground
   black pepper

If vegetarian inspiration evades you, this aromatic, full-flavoured recipe is a good one to have up your sleeve. Serve with plain yoghurt, infused with chopped fresh mint, a little salt and ground roasted cumin.

1 For the filling, halve and peel the onions, then slice thinly into half rings. Deseed the pepper and cut into thin slices. Finely chop the apricots. Peel and crush the garlic. Drain and rinse the chickpeas and wash the spinach. Roughly chop the fresh coriander. Set everything aside, in separate bowls.

2 Heat the oil in a medium saucepan, add the onions, cover with a damp cartouche (see page 155) and a lid and sweat over a low heat until soft, checking regularly that they don't begin to brown.

3 Remove the cartouche and add the red pepper to the onions. Cook until the pepper begins to soften, then add the garlic and continue to cook for 1 minute, stirring. Add the tomato purée, harissa, coriander and cumin seeds, crushed dried chillies, paprika and cinnamon. Mix well and cook for 1–2 minutes.

4 Add the tomatoes and apricots to the pan, stir well and simmer gently, uncovered, for 10–15 minutes, to drive off excess liquid and concentrate the flavour. When the mixture is moist but not runny, add the chickpeas and spinach and heat through until the spinach is just wilted.

5 Add the chopped coriander and two thirds of the flaked almonds. Season with salt and pepper, remove from the heat and set aside to cool.

6 Meanwhile, heat the oven to 200°C/gas mark 6. Melt the butter and grease a large baking sheet.

7 Gently stretch the strudel pastry on a floured tea towel to a large rectangle (see page 106) and trim the edges with a large knife. If using bought filo, arrange overlapping sheets on a floured tea towel to make a rectangle approximately 30 x 40cm.

8 Brush the pastry with the melted butter and place the chickpea filling in a line down the short edge of the pastry, leaving a 2cm border. Using the tea towel to help, roll the pastry around the filling, in a fairly tight roll, brushing off any excess flour as you roll. Lift the cloth and gently tip the strudel onto the prepared baking sheet, with the pastry join underneath.

9 Brush the pastry with more butter and sprinkle over the remaining almonds, then bake in the middle of the oven for 25–30 minutes, or until the pastry is golden brown and the filling is piping hot. Remove from the oven and transfer to a warm serving dish.

AUBERGINE AND POMEGRANATE STRUDEL TARTLETS

MAKES 40 canapé tartlets

100g butter
1 quantity strudel pastry
 (see page 106) or 6–8
 sheets of bought filo

FOR THE FILLING
2 medium aubergines
1 pomegranate
Small bunch of mint
3 tbsp sunflower oil
175g natural yoghurt
1 lemon
Salt and freshly ground
 black pepper

To shape these delicate, bite-sized tartlets, you will need a mini muffin tray. Alternatively, for a starter, use individual tart cases and serve the tartlets garnished with mint leaves and served with a dollop of Greek yoghurt rippled through with a spoonful of pomegranate molasses.

1 For the filling, cut the aubergines into 0.5–1cm dice. To remove the seeds from the pomegranate, roll it on the work surface to loosen the seeds, cut it in half and bash the rounded end with a wooden spoon over a bowl to catch the seeds. Pick the mint leaves and chiffonade (finely slice) them.

2 Heat a large frying pan until very hot. Add the oil and then the diced aubergines. Fry until a deep golden colour, stirring occasionally. Season with salt and pepper, then transfer to a plate and cover with cling film. Leave for 10 minutes to soften.

3 Mix the softened aubergine with the yoghurt, mint and pomegranate seeds. Add lemon juice, salt and pepper to taste. Heat the oven to 180°C/gas mark 4.

4 Melt the butter in a small saucepan. Lay out the pastry on a work surface and stretch it until it is nearly paper thin (see page 106). Trim off the thicker edges, then cut into 5cm squares, working quite quickly as the strudel pastry will become dry and brittle if exposed to the air for too long. If you are using filo, use one piece at a time and make sure the rest of the packet is well wrapped.

5 Take one of the pastry squares and brush with the melted butter. Lay a second square on top, offset by roughly 30°. Brush with butter before adding a third square of pastry, again offset by roughly 30°. Brush this top square with butter and then mould the pastry stack into one of the holes of a mini muffin tray to form a little cup.

6 Repeat with the remaining pastry squares. Bake in the oven for 5–6 minutes until light golden and crisp, then remove to a wire rack and leave to cool. You will probably need to bake the pastry cases in batches, and take care as they burn easily.

7 Spoon or pipe the aubergine mixture into the tart cases shortly before serving.

DATE AND FETA STRUDEL

SERVES 6

85g unsalted butter
3 tbsp poppy seeds
Finely grated zest of
    1½ lemons
1 quantity strudel pastry
    (see page 106) or 6–8
    sheets of bought filo
Extra flour, to dust

FOR THE FILLING
3 banana shallots
250g stoneless Medjool dates

60g pine nuts
1½ tbsp sunflower oil
2 tbsp water
3 tbsp Moscatel vinegar
250g feta cheese, crumbled
Salt and freshly ground
    black pepper

TO FINISH
1 egg
1 tbsp poppy seeds

This Middle Eastern inspired savoury strudel has an enticing sweet/salty flavour thanks to the unusual combination of crumbled feta and sweet dates. It looks particularly beautiful if shaped into a golden glazed coil of pastry. Delicious served with a lightly dressed salad as a starter.

1 To make the filling, halve, peel and very finely chop the shallots. Roughly chop the dates. Roughly chop the pine nuts and set aside in separate bowls.

2 Heat the oil in a small saucepan over a low heat. Add the shallots and sweat for 10 minutes, or until soft and transparent. Increase the heat to medium, add the chopped dates, water and vinegar and cook for 1 minute. Season with a little salt and pepper, reduce the heat, cover and cook gently for 10 minutes or until the dates are soft and pulpy. The mixture should be a fairly thick paste, so increase the heat and boil rapidly for a few seconds, uncovered, if there is any excess moisture.

3 Remove from the heat and, while the mixture is still hot, crumble in the feta and add the pine nuts. Stir carefully to combine, trying not to break up the feta too much. Transfer to a bowl and leave to cool completely. Meanwhile, heat the oven to 200°C/gas mark 6.

4 Melt the butter in a small saucepan over a low heat. Stir in the poppy seeds and lemon zest, remove from the heat and set aside to cool a little.

5 Stretch the pastry out to a 30cm square (see page 106), trim the edges with a large knife and lay on a floured tea towel. If using bought filo, arrange overlapping sheets on a floured tea towel to make a 30cm square. Brush the pastry generously with the melted butter, then spread the date and feta mixture evenly over the surface of the buttered pastry.

6 Using the tea towel to help, roll up the pastry in a fairly tight roll. Gently tip the strudel onto a baking sheet, with the pastry join underneath. Shape into a coil, firmly tucking the end piece underneath to secure the shape, or simply bend the strudel into a horseshoe shape, which will also cook a little faster.

7 Using a fork, beat the egg with a pinch of salt and pass through a sieve into a bowl. Brush the strudel with the beaten egg and sprinkle with poppy seeds.

8 Bake in the top third of the oven for 30–40 minutes, or until the pastry is crisp and a deep golden colour. Check that the centre of the coil is cooked through and the pastry feels dry to the touch. Transfer to a wire rack and leave to cool slightly before serving warm.

APPLE STRUDEL

SERVES 6

1 quantity strudel pastry
   (see page 106) or 6–8
   sheets of bought filo
Extra flour, to dust
100g butter
Icing sugar, to dust

FOR THE FILLING
1kg Bramley apples
1 lemon
100g raisins
60g soft light brown sugar
½ tsp ground cinnamon
Pinch of ground cloves
2–3 tbsp dried breadcrumbs

This famous Austrian strudel is a lovely way to use a glut of Bramleys in the autumn. Serve hot with custard, or cold with cream.

1 Heat the oven to 220°C/gas mark 7.

2 For the filling, peel, quarter and core the apples, then cut into irregular 2.5cm chunks. Place in a bowl.

3 Finely grate the zest and squeeze the juice of half the lemon, then add to the apples with the raisins, sugar and spices, and mix together well. The earlier you make the filling the better, as the flavours will combine and the sharp edges of the apple will soften. Taste and add more sugar and spices if necessary; the filling should be sweet rather than sharp, but not cloyingly so.

4 If using homemade strudel pastry, gently stretch it on a floured tea towel into a large rectangle (see page 106) and trim the edges with a large knife. If using bought filo, overlap the sheets to make a rectangle about 30 x 40cm. Melt the butter in a small saucepan and use to brush the pastry, then scatter the breadcrumbs over the surface.

5 Place three quarters of the filling along one short end of the pastry and scatter the remaining filling over the surface.

6 Using the tea towel to help, roll up the pastry from a short edge in a fairly tight roll, brushing off the excess flour as you go. Roll the strudel onto a baking sheet, with the pastry join underneath, and curve into a half moon shape. Dust off the excess flour and brush with melted butter.

7 Bake in the oven for 30–40 minutes until the pastry is a deep golden colour and crisp. The apples should be soft; use a skewer to check.

8 Trim off the pastry ends and carefully transfer the strudel to a serving platter. Dust with icing sugar and serve warm or cold.

Variation

❋ **Pear and Medjool date strudel** Replace the apples, raisins, sugar, cinnamon and cloves with 1kg pears, peeled, cored and cut into chunks, 200g Medjool dates, pitted and cut into chunks, ¼ tsp freshly grated peeled ginger and 30g soft dark brown sugar.

5

CHOUX PASTRY

Choux pastry is unlike other pastries in its method, in that it is cooked twice and is not affected by the heat of your hands or the kitchen. It is a really versatile pastry; it can be made into savoury or sweet dishes and cooked to any size or shape without needing moulds and tins. It can be baked or deep-fried, the dough itself can be flavoured, and it produces the perfect crisp container for any sweet or savoury filling. It also has the benefit of being surprisingly easy to make once you know how.

The two key tips to making good choux are to make sure you weigh everything out accurately, and to ensure the water is hot enough when adding the flour.

CHOUX PASTRY

MAKES 1 quantity	
220ml water	Pinch of salt
85g butter	3 eggs, at room temperature
105g plain flour	

1 Measure the water into a small saucepan. Cut the butter into 1cm cubes and add to the water. Place over a low heat and allow the butter to melt, without letting the water simmer or boil (which would result in less liquid, through evaporation, and a stiff mixture that won't rise as well).

2 Meanwhile, sift the flour and salt 2 or 3 times to aerate it and remove any lumps. Do the final sifting onto a sheet of greaseproof paper. Fold the paper in half and fold up the bottom edge a couple of times to create a pocket for the flour to sit in. (This will make it easier to add it all at once to the water and butter.)

3 Once the butter has melted, increase the heat to medium-high and have the pocket of flour and a wooden spoon close by. As the water begins to simmer, watch it carefully and, as it boils and rises up the sides of the pan, with the melted butter collecting in the middle, shoot the flour in all at once and turn off the heat.

4 Beat the flour in vigorously for just 20–30 seconds, getting the spoon into the corners of the saucepan, until the flour is fully incorporated, there are no lumps and the mixture is thick and a uniform colour. Spread this panade onto a plate and let it cool until tepid (about 38°C). Cooling the panade will allow the incorporation of more egg, to ensure a greater rise.

5 Meanwhile, break the eggs into a bowl and whisk lightly with a fork. Once the panade is cool to the touch, return it to the saucepan (there's no need to wash it), add about 1 tbsp of the beaten egg and beat it into the panade with a wooden spoon (off the heat). Once the egg is fully incorporated, add a little more egg and beat again, adding about three quarters of the remaining egg in additions and beating well to incorporate each addition fully before the next. Initially, the panade will thicken, but as more egg is beaten in it will start to loosen and become smooth and shiny.

6 Once about three quarters of the egg has been added, check the consistency; you need a silky smooth pastry with a reluctant dropping consistency, which means that when you fill the wooden spoon with pastry and lift it up over the saucepan the pastry should fall back from the spoon into the saucepan to the slow count of six. Continue adding egg a little at a time until the correct consistency is achieved. The pastry can now be used, or covered and either stored in the fridge overnight or frozen.

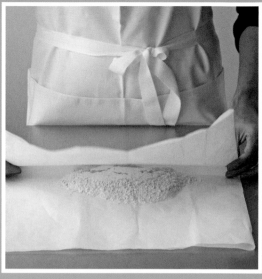

1 Adding the butter to the water to melt.

2 Folding the sheet of paper to enclose the flour and contain it in a pocket.

3 Shooting the flour into the boiling water and butter mixture.

(Continued overleaf)

A note on beating in the flour...

✳ Beating the flour in for just 20–30 seconds is very important, as any longer and the panade may become greasy and look split, creating slightly greasy cooked pastry and an unattractive cracked surface.

4 Spreading the panade out on a plate to cool.

5 Incorporating the beaten egg into the panade a little at a time (off the heat).

A note on adding the egg...

✻ If too little egg is added, the choux pastry will not rise successfully. If too much egg is added, the choux will be too loose to hold its shape and it may struggle to rise. So 3 eggs in the recipe is a guide only; you need to add just enough to achieve a reluctant dropping consistency.

The egg can be incorporated using a hand-held electric whisk if preferred, still in several additions and taking care not to add too much.

CHEDDAR AND CHIVE BEIGNETS

MAKES 20–24

220ml water
85g butter
105g plain flour
¼ tsp smoked paprika
¼ tsp English mustard
   powder

¼ tsp cayenne pepper
3 eggs
100g strong Cheddar cheese
¼ bunch of chives
Oil, for deep-frying
Salt

These can be served as canapés or to accompany soups. Tiny beignets like these can be made in all manner of flavours, so experiment with adding other ingredients; just make sure any additions are not too wet or the beignets won't hold their shape.

1 Measure the water into a small saucepan. Cut the butter into 1cm cubes and add to the water. Place over a low heat to melt the butter, without letting the water simmer or boil.

2 Meanwhile, sift the flour, a pinch of salt and the spices 2 or 3 times to aerate and remove any lumps, doing the last sifting onto a sheet of greaseproof paper. Fold the paper to create a pocket for the flour (see step 2, page 118).

3 Once the butter has melted, increase the heat to medium-high. As the water begins to boil and rises up the sides of the pan, shoot the flour in, remove from the heat and beat vigorously for just 20–30 seconds, until the flour is fully incorporated, there are no lumps and the panade is a uniform colour and coming away from the side of the pan (see step 4, page 118).

4 Spread the panade onto a plate to allow it to cool to tepid (about 38°C).

5 Break the eggs into a bowl and whisk lightly with a fork.

6 Once the panade is cool to the touch, return it to the pan and beat 1 tbsp egg in vigorously, using a wooden spoon. Once the egg is fully incorporated, add a little more egg and beat again. Continue to add about three quarters of the remaining egg in this way, beating well to incorporate each addition before adding the next. Initially the panade will thicken, but as more egg is beaten in it will start to loosen and become smooth and shiny.

7 Check the consistency is a reluctant dropping consistency (see step 6, page 118). If it is too stiff, continue to add egg in small additions until the correct consistency is achieved, but don't add too much or the choux won't hold its shape and will struggle to rise.

8 Finely grate the cheese and finely chop the chives, then stir both well into the choux pastry.

9 Heat the oil in a deep-fat fryer or large saucepan half-filled with oil, to 195°C, or until a small piece of bread dropped into the oil browns in 25 seconds. Using 2 lightly oiled teaspoons, drop spoonfuls of the choux into the hot oil, a few at a time.

10 As the beignets heat up, tap them lightly with a spoon and they should expand and puff up. Deep-fry for about 5 minutes until golden brown, crisp and cooked through. Remove the beignets with a slotted spoon and drain on kitchen paper, then sprinkle with a little salt and serve warm.

Variations

✱ **Blue cheese and sage beignets** Replace the Cheddar and chives with 75–100g finely crumbled blue cheese and 2–3 finely shredded sage leaves.

✱ **Crab, chilli and coriander beignets** Omit the Cheddar and chives. Add 50g white crab meat and 25g brown crab meat with a finely diced, deseeded red chilli and 1 tbsp chopped coriander.

✱ All the above beignets can be baked in the oven, preheated to 200°C/gas mark 6, for 10–15 minutes rather than deep-fried. They are cooked when golden brown and firm to the touch.

SMOKED TROUT
AND DILL GOUGÈRE

SERVES 4

75g Gruyère cheese
1 quantity choux pastry
   (see page 118, adding
   a pinch each of English
   mustard powder and
   cayenne to the flour)

FOR THE FILLING
6 hot smoked trout fillets or
   3 whole smoked trout,
   filleted

¼ bunch of dill
125ml crème fraîche
30–40ml double cream
1–2 tsp creamed horseradish
Salt and freshly ground
   black pepper

TO FINISH
1 tbsp white breadcrumbs

A gougère is cheese-flavoured choux pastry with a savoury filling. For this recipe you will need a 1 litre ovenproof dish, 4–5cm deep.

1 Cut 50g of the Gruyère into small dice, grate the remaining 25g and set aside. Heat the oven to 200°C/gas mark 6.

2 Stir the diced Gruyère into the choux pastry mixture.

3 Spoon or pipe the choux around the edges of a shallow, greased ovenproof dish, about 30 x 30cm and 4–5cm deep (about 1 litre in volume), leaving a space for the filling in the centre. Bake for 35–45 minutes, or until well risen, a deep golden colour and very firm to the touch at the sides.

4 Meanwhile, to make the filling, pin bone the trout fillets and break into large flakes or pieces in a bowl. Finely chop enough dill to give you 1–1½ tbsp.

5 In a small bowl, mix together the crème fraîche, double cream and 1–2 tsp creamed horseradish to taste, then add the dill to taste. Add this mixture to the trout, taste and adjust the seasoning with salt and black pepper.

6 When the choux pastry is cooked, remove from the oven and lower the oven temperature to 180°C/gas mark 4. If the pastry has risen towards the middle of the dish, push this aside a little to allow room for the filling.

7 Spoon the filling into the centre of the choux and return to the oven to warm through; this will take 20–25 minutes.

Mix the breadcrumbs with the reserved grated Gruyère. About 5–10 minutes before the gougère is due to come out of the oven, turn the oven setting up to 200°C/gas mark 6 and sprinkle the cheese and breadcrumbs over the filling. Continue to bake until golden and the crumb topping is lightly browned. Serve hot or warm.

Variations

✻ **Leek and mushroom gougère** Omit the smoked trout and dill filling. Thinly slice 2 cleaned, large leeks. Slice 75g button mushrooms. Heat 2 tbsp olive oil in a large frying pan over a low heat, add the leeks, cover and sweat until soft and translucent. Add the mushrooms and 1–2 tsp chopped thyme, and sauté until soft. Add 75ml white wine, bring to the boil and let bubble for 2–3 minutes. Remove from the heat, stir in 150ml crème fraîche and season to taste with salt and pepper. Use to fill the gougère and bake as for the main recipe.

✻ **Individual gougères** Gougères can be made in individual ramekins. The quantity of choux in the main recipe will make 8 individual gougères, in standard 7.5–8cm diameter ramekins. Follow the above method but cut and shred the ingredients for the filling into smaller pieces. You don't need to pre-bake the gougère before filling. They will take about 30 minutes to cook; the choux will rise around the filling and give a softer result.

PASSION FRUIT ÉCLAIRS

MAKES 20 small or 12–15 large éclairs

Sunflower oil, to grease
1 quantity choux pastry (see page 118)

FOR THE FILLING
2 x quantity crème pâtissière (see page 152)

FOR THE TOPPING
6 ripe passion fruit or 2–4 tbsp passion fruit purée (ready-made)
250g icing sugar

Éclairs lend themselves to various tempting fillings and toppings and make delightful teatime treats.

1 Heat the oven to 200°C/gas mark 6. Very lightly oil a non-stick baking sheet.

2 Scoop the choux pastry into a piping bag fitted with a plain 7–8mm nozzle and pipe the choux onto the baking sheet into flat 'S' shapes (with no gaps), 7–8cm long, spacing them about 4–5cm apart. Use a lightly dampened, clean finger to smooth out any spikes or peaks.

3 Bake in the top third of the oven for 25–35 minutes until well risen and puffed, and a deep golden brown all over, checking after 25 minutes (no earlier or they may collapse). They should be very firm to the touch on the base. If they are pale golden and soft, bake them for longer.

4 Remove from the oven and reduce the oven temperature to 170°C/gas mark 3. While the pastry is still hot, use a skewer to make a hole in both ends of the éclair, about 5mm in diameter or the size of your small piping nozzle, for the steam to escape. Place the éclairs back on the baking sheet and return to the oven for 5–6 minutes to dry the insides; they should be really crisp. Transfer to a wire rack to cool completely before filling.

5 For the filling, briefly blitz the crème pâtissière in a food processor to ensure it is smooth. Transfer to a piping bag fitted with a small nozzle. Take one éclair in your palm and pipe the crème pâtissière into one of the holes, holding the piping bag vertically. Repeat to fill the rest of the éclairs.

6 For the topping, cut the passion fruit, if using, in half and scoop out the insides. Pulse just briefly in a food processor (or the seeds will start to break up). Sieve the juice into a small bowl. Sift the icing sugar into a bowl and beat with enough of the passion fruit juice, or purée, to make a smooth icing.

7 Dip each éclair top into the icing to coat and place on a plate. Alternatively, you can spoon the topping onto the éclairs to coat them evenly.

Variations

* **Raspberry or blackcurrant** Fill the éclairs with crème pâtissière (replacing 50ml of the milk with raspberry or blackcurrant purée if you wish). For the topping, sift 250g icing sugar into a bowl and mix in enough raspberry or blackcurrant purée (3–4 tbsp) to form a thick glacé icing. Dip in the filled éclairs or spoon the icing over the top.

* **Pistachio or other nut** Fill the éclairs with crème pâtissière (replacing 1–2 tbsp of the milk with pistachio paste if you wish). For the topping, sift 250g icing sugar into a bowl and mix in enough boiling water to make a thick glacé icing. Use to top the éclairs, then immediately sprinkle with 150g lightly toasted, chopped pistachio nuts.

* **Coffee** Fill the éclairs with 600ml double cream whipped with 2 tbsp icing sugar. For the topping, sift the icing sugar into a large bowl and beat in enough hot espresso (2–3 tbsp) to make a thick glacé icing.

* **Chocolate** Fill the éclairs with crème pâtissière or lightly sweetened whipped cream (as for coffee éclairs). Make the topping as for chocolate profiteroles (see page 126) and use to coat the éclairs.

CHOCOLATE PROFITEROLES

Sunflower oil, to grease
1 quantity choux pastry
   (see page 118)

FOR THE FILLING
600ml double cream
2 tbsp icing sugar

FOR THE TOPPING
250g good quality dark
   chocolate, minimum
   60% cocoa solids
2 tbsp water
15g butter

The perfect profiterole is completely filled with sweet cream and liberally topped with glossy chocolate, so be generous when filling and coating your profiteroles.

1 Heat the oven to 200°C/gas mark 6. Very lightly oil a non-stick baking sheet.

2 Put teaspoonfuls of the choux pastry onto the prepared baking sheet, spacing them about 4–5cm apart. (They need plenty of room to rise as if 2 buns join while rising they can make each other collapse.) Use a dampened, clean finger to smooth out any spikes or peaks on the choux buns.

3 Bake in the top third of the oven for 20–30 minutes until well risen and puffed, and a deep golden brown all over, checking after 20 minutes (no earlier or they may collapse). The buns should also be very firm to the touch on the base where they sit on the baking tray; if soft and pale golden, cook for longer.

4 Take out the buns and lower the oven setting to 170°C/gas mark 3. While hot, turn each choux bun over and use a skewer to make a hole in the base, about 5mm (the size of your smallest piping nozzle), to allow the steam to escape. Place the buns, base up, on the baking sheet and return to the oven for 5–6 minutes to dry the insides. Transfer to a wire rack to cool.

5 While the choux buns are cooling, for the topping, break the chocolate into pieces and put into a small heatproof bowl with the water and butter. Set over a saucepan of just-boiled water, ensuring the bowl is not touching the water. Give it an occasional stir to encourage melting.

6 For the filling, put the cream and icing sugar into a large bowl. Whisk to a pipeable consistency, then place in a piping bag fitted with a small (5mm) nozzle.

7 When the profiteroles are completely cold, take one in the palm of a clean hand and pipe the cream into the hole. Once filled, scrape away any escaping cream and return to the wire rack. Repeat with all the profiteroles.

8 Hold one profiterole upside down at its base, using your fingertips, and turn the top of the profiterole through the melted chocolate, keeping your fingers clear of the chocolate. Carefully turn the profiterole over and place on a serving plate. Repeat with the remaining profiteroles.

Variations

✱ You can fill the profiteroles with crème pâtissière (see page 152) instead of cream.

✱ Rather than dip in melted chocolate, serve the profiteroles with a hot chocolate sauce. Melt together 170g dark chocolate, 4 tbsp water, 1 tsp instant coffee powder, 1 tbsp golden syrup and 15g butter in a small pan over a low heat, stirring. Pour the sauce over the cream-filled profiteroles and serve at once.

A note on freezing...

✱ Choux buns, profiteroles and éclairs can be frozen in an airtight container once cooked, before they are filled. Store for up to a few months, defrosting them overnight in the fridge. Warm through on a baking sheet in an oven preheated to 190°C/gas mark 5 for 5–10 minutes to crisp them up again.

APPLE AND CINNAMON BEIGNETS

750g Bramleys, or other
cooking apples
About 60g caster sugar
Oil, for deep-frying
1 quantity choux pastry
(see page 118)

**FOR THE BLACKBERRY
SAUCE**
250g blackberries
About 70g caster sugar
1 tbsp water

TO SERVE
2 tsp ground cinnamon
10g caster sugar

**These are incredibly more-ish, and a wonderful way
to showcase blackberries when they are abundant.**

1 Peel and core the apples and cut into even 5mm dice.
Put into a saucepan with the 60g sugar, cover with a damp
cartouche (see page 155) and cook over a gentle heat until
softening, but still retaining a little texture. Keep an eye on
them as they cook, adding a little water if they dry out. Remove
from the heat and taste while still warm, adding a little extra
sugar if the mixture is too tart. Set aside in the pan.

2 For the blackberry sauce, put the blackberries in a saucepan
with the sugar and water. Cook over a very gentle heat until
they release their juices to create a sauce, but are not breaking
down completely. Taste and add more sugar if necessary to
balance the flavour, then set aside in the pan.

3 Heat the oil in a deep-fat fryer or large saucepan half filled
with oil to 195°C, or until a small piece of bread dropped into
the oil browns in 25 seconds.

4 Using lightly oiled teaspoons, drop spoonfuls of choux into
the hot oil, in batches of no more than 6. Cook for 3–4 minutes
until well expanded and evenly golden. They should increase
to around 3 times their original size; tapping them gently with
a large metal spoon encourages their expansion.

5 Remove the cooked beignets to kitchen paper to drain,
allowing them to cool slightly while you cook the remaining
mixture in batches.

6 Meanwhile, reheat the apple gently, and carefully pour into
a disposable piping bag without a nozzle (or a piping bag fitted
with a nozzle of about 5mm so the pieces of apple will just
squeeze through), supporting the piping bag in a measuring
jug to prevent the hot apple coming out of the open end.

7 Mix the ground cinnamon with the 10g sugar in a bowl.

8 Use a skewer to make a hole about 5mm wide in the
underside of each beignet. Using a pair of scissors, cut an
opening at the nozzle end of the piping bag of no larger
than 5mm. With the apple mixture still warm, carefully pipe
it into the beignets through the holes, making sure they are
generously filled.

9 Toss each filled beignet through the cinnamon sugar until
evenly coated. Serve at once, while still warm, with the
blackberry sauce and some vanilla ice cream.

LEMON CHOUX FEUILLETTÉS

MAKES 12

Sunflower oil, to grease
1 quantity choux pastry
  (see page 118)

FOR THE FILLING
250ml double cream
1 tbsp icing sugar, plus
  extra to dust
200ml homemade or good
  quality bought lemon curd

This is an unusual way of using choux pastry, and is a delicious teatime treat. They are also very good filled with fresh berries and cream flavoured with vanilla.

1 Heat the oven to 200°C/gas mark 6. Lightly oil 2 large baking sheets.

2 Place 1 heaped tablespoonful of choux pastry on the baking sheet and use a palette knife to spread it out to a 10cm circle, about 3mm thick. With a wet finger, tidy the shape and scrape off any excess mixture.

3 Repeat with the remaining choux, leaving a 2cm gap between circles, until both baking sheets are filled. You may need to cook the choux circles in 2 batches, depending on the size of the baking sheets.

4 Bake for 10 minutes, then lower the oven setting to 180°C/gas mark 4 and cook for a further 10–15 minutes, or until the circles have risen, are golden brown and completely crisp. Remove to a wire rack and leave to cool completely.

5 Put the cream in a bowl, sift in the 1 tbsp icing sugar and lightly whip until it just holds its shape.

6 Sandwich 2 cooled choux circles together with 1 tbsp of the sweetened cream and 1 tbsp lemon curd, either in 2 separate spoonfuls or lightly stirred together to give a marbled effect. Repeat with the remaining choux, sprinkle with icing sugar and serve.

6

HOT WATER CRUST PASTRY

Hot water crust pastry is traditionally used for raised pies. It is an unusual pastry, similar to choux in that the fat and water are heated before mixing with the flour, although hot water crust pastry doesn't rise when baked, and can be said to be twice cooked. Ideally, making the pastry and shaping the case should be done a day ahead to allow the pastry time to firm up before filling and baking.

HOT WATER CRUST PASTRY

MAKES enough for a raised pie to serve 6–8

150ml water
60g butter
60g lard

350g plain flour
¾ tsp salt
1 large egg

1 Put the water into a medium saucepan. Cut the butter and lard into 1cm cubes and add these to the pan. Place over a low heat and melt the fats; the water must not boil before they have melted.

2 Meanwhile, sift the flour and salt into a large bowl and make a well in the middle. Break the egg into a small bowl, beat lightly with a fork and pour into the well. Carefully flick flour over the egg to protect it from the hot water and fats.

3 Once the fats have melted, increase the heat and bring to the boil. As it comes to a rolling boil, take off the heat, pour over the flour in the bowl and immediately mix everything together well with a cutlery knife, until you can no longer see any dry flour. The pastry should be warm and greasy to the touch. Bring it together in your hands until smooth, then divide into 2 pieces, one twice the size of the other.

4 Shape the smaller piece of pastry into a disc, 10–12cm in diameter, and the larger piece into a disc, 15–18cm in diameter. The discs should be smooth, with no cracks or pleats. Wrap both individually in cling film and chill for 45–60 minutes for the fats to firm up.

To shape a raised pie...

The aim here is to make a watertight container in which meat is cooked in the oven with just a band of baking parchment around the sides as support. The pastry must be thick enough to withstand the weight of the meat, but not so thick that it is unpleasant to eat. It must not have any weak points, or be too thin, or the pie will collapse. It is therefore important that the original shaping of the warm pastry into a disc creates no pleats, and that when shaping round the dish it is not forced or pushed too hard, which could cause it to crack or break. While the pastry is chilling, prepare the mould for the raised pie. Traditionally, a wooden mould is used. A large 400ml soufflé dish, 12.5cm in diameter, works well. (Individual pies can be raised without moulds.)

1 Cut a disc of greaseproof paper for the outside base of the dish and a band to go around the outside walls of the dish. Stick the greaseproof paper to the outside of the dish using sticky tape. Now place the dish on a large sheet of cling film and bring the cling film up the sides of the dish and down into it, pulling it so it is taut. The soufflé dish is now ready for the pastry.

2 Remove the larger disc of pastry from the fridge; it should be firm, but pliable. Turn the soufflé dish upside down and lay the pastry across the upturned base. Gently ease the pastry down the sides of the dish. The warmth from your hands will help to soften the pastry a little and make it easier to mould. Avoid pushing too firmly or the pastry will crack. Roll a rolling pin lightly across the top of the dish or use your hands flat against the top, to encourage the pastry to expand and ease down the sides of the dish.

3 With your fingers flat against the side of the dish, gently ease the pastry down (as shown). You need to work on the top and sides alternately to coat the dish all over in an even layer of pastry. Avoid using your fingers over the corners of the dish as this can easily create a thin layer of pastry. Place uncovered on a tray in the fridge for 5–6 hours, or ideally overnight, for it to firm even more and dry out.

PORK, APPLE AND SAGE RAISED PIE

| **SERVES** 4 |

1 quantity hot water crust
    pastry (see page 132)
1 egg

FOR THE FILLING
1 small onion
5–6 sage leaves, or 1 tsp
    dried sage

650g boned shoulder of pork
1 dessert apple
30g raisins
150–200ml aspic
    (see opposite)
Salt and freshly ground
    black pepper

You will need a 400ml soufflé dish to shape this pie.

1 Prepare and shape the pastry around a 400ml soufflé dish (see page 132).

2 The next day, or when ready to cook, heat the oven to 190°C/gas mark 5.

3 For the filling, halve, peel and finely dice the onion. Finely chop the fresh sage leaves, if using. Remove any sinew and trim any excess fat off the pork, then cut into 1.5cm cubes. Peel, core and finely dice the apple.

4 Mix the onion, pork, apple, raisins and half the sage together in a large bowl and season well with salt and plenty of pepper. Reserve the rest of the sage for the aspic.

5 Remove the shaped pastry and the smaller disc from the fridge. Turn the shaped pastry the right way up and peel the cling film away from inside the dish. Ease the cling film a little from the dish and lift the dish out of the pastry (as shown opposite) without damaging the pastry. Peel away the cling film and greaseproof paper from the inside of the pastry case.

6 Carefully lift the pastry case up to the light and check the corners; if you can see light through them you will need to reinforce them using a thin band cut from around the edge of the pastry for the lid, by gently pushing it into the area needed.

7 Wrap a double layer of baking parchment around the outside of the pie case to support it and secure with paper clips or string (don't tie string too tightly or it will create a waist in the pie once cooked). Make sure the rim of pastry is not covered by paper, so you can seal it with the lid.

8 Place the pie case on a lipped baking sheet and add the filling, packing it into the corners, to help support the pastry, and doming it on the top.

9 Check the pastry lid is the right size to fit over the top. Lightly beat the egg with a very small pinch of salt, using a fork, then pass through a sieve into a bowl. Brush beaten egg on the inside of the pastry lid. Lay the lid on top of the pie, fold the edges of the lid up against the inside of the pie and press together to seal. Using a pair of scissors, trim off only the top edge, not too deep or you will break the seal.

10 Using your thumb and forefinger, crimp the pastry edge. Now make a steam hole in the middle of the top and insert the tip of a 5mm piping nozzle (this will prevent the hole closing). If you have any pastry left, roll it out thinly and cut out decorations, if desired; stick them to the top of the pie with the beaten egg.

11 Brush the top of the pie with beaten egg to glaze. Bake for 15 minutes, then lower the oven setting to 170°C/gas mark 3 and bake the pie for a further 30 minutes. Remove from the oven and take off the paper collar. If the pie suddenly begins to slump and lose shape, tie the paper round the pie again and continue to cook for a further 15 minutes. If the pie holds its shape, brush the sides and the top again with beaten egg and return to the oven for a further 30 minutes, or until cooked.

12 To check that the pie is cooked, insert a skewer into the middle through the steam hole, leave it for 10 seconds, then remove and immediately touch it to your inner wrist; it should be hot. If not, cook the pie for a further 15 minutes.

13 Once the pie is cooked, remove it from the oven and set aside to cool to room temperature.

14 Follow the instructions on the aspic packet to dissolve and sponge it. When the aspic begins to thicken and set a little (still pourable but thick enough to hold the sage in suspension), add the reserved sage.

15 Carefully pour the aspic through the piping nozzle into the pie (as shown), allowing it to seep into the air holes and between the meat and the pastry. You might need to lift the pastry around the steam hole first to allow the aspic to feed through, taking care not to break the pastry. Allow the aspic to set for 3–4 hours before cutting the pie.

· ·

Variations

✳ **Veal and ham raised pie** Replace the filling with 550g cubed shoulder of veal, 100g cubed gammon, 1 small finely diced onion and a bunch of parsley, finely chopped. Season well.

✳ **Duck and green peppercorn raised pie** Replace the filling with 150g cubed shoulder of veal and 400g cubed duck leg meat (about 3–4 duck legs, meat only, sinews removed) tossed in 1½ tbsp cornflour, 1 small finely diced onion, ½–1 tbsp green peppercorns, lightly crushed, and a bunch of parsley, finely chopped. Season well with salt and pepper.

✳ **Individual raised pies** Shape the pastry around ramekins and proceed as for the main recipe, or shape the cases by hand.

A note on leakage...

Raised pies can sometimes leak, if the pastry is a little thin or has a weak spot. If after cooking the pie is leaking, allow it to cool, then use soft butter to plug any holes.

Allow the butter to firm completely by putting the pie in the fridge for 30–45 minutes. After the aspic has been added to the pie and set, the butter can be scraped away before serving.

· ·

A note on aspic...

Aspic is added to raised pies because as the meat cooks it shrinks and releases juices, and as it cools the meat re-absorbs the juice but leaves a gap between the meat and the pastry walls of the pie. Aspic fills all the air holes and holds the pie together when cut. It also helps to preserve the pie, so it can be kept for a few days.

Traditionally, the bones from the meat would be simmered in water and flavourings, strained and cooled to produce a savoury jelly. But these days you can buy aspic powder and use it in the same way as gelatine.

Alternatively, you can use gelatine: 1 tsp powdered gelatine is enough to soft-set 150–200ml lightly flavoured chicken stock. Add a little tarragon or sherry vinegar (about 1 tsp or to taste), 1 tsp finely chopped parsley and salt and pepper.

RAISED GAME PIE

1 quantity hot water crust
    pastry (see page 132)
1 egg

FOR THE FILLING
1 small onion
350g boned mixed game
    (such as venison, rabbit,
    pheasant and/or pigeon)

3 rashers of streaky bacon
5–6 sage leaves, or 1 tsp
    dried sage
250g minced belly pork
¼ tsp ground allspice
150–200ml aspic
    (see page 135)
Salt and freshly ground
    black pepper

You will need a 400ml soufflé dish to shape this pie.

1 Prepare and shape the pastry around a 400ml soufflé dish (see page 132).

2 The next day, or when ready to cook, heat the oven to 190°C/ gas mark 5.

3 For the filling, halve, peel and finely dice the onion. Remove any sinew from the game, then cut into 1.5cm cubes. Derind the bacon and cut into strips. Finely chop the fresh sage, if using.

4 Mix the onion, game, minced pork, bacon, allspice and half the sage together in a large bowl and season well with salt and plenty of pepper. Reserve the rest of the sage for the aspic.

5 Remove the shaped pastry and the smaller disc from the fridge. Turn the shaped pastry the right way up and peel the cling film away from inside the dish. Ease the cling film a little from the dish and lift the dish out of the pastry (as shown on page 135) without damaging the pastry. Peel away the cling film and greaseproof paper from the inside of the pastry case.

6 Carefully lift the pastry case up to the light and check the corners; if you can see light through them you will need to reinforce them using a thin band cut from around the edge of the pastry for the lid, by gently pushing it into the area needed.

7 Wrap a double layer of baking parchment around the outside of the pie case to support it and secure with paper clips or string (don't tie string too tightly or it will create a waist in the pie once cooked). Make sure the rim of pastry is not covered by paper, so you can seal it with the lid.

8 Place the pie case on a lipped baking sheet and add the filling, packing it into the corners and doming it on the top.

9 Check the pastry lid is the right size to fit over the top. Lightly beat the egg with a very small pinch of salt, using a fork, then pass through a sieve into a bowl. Brush beaten egg on the inside of the pastry lid. Lay the lid on top of the pie, fold the edges of the lid up against the inside of the pie and press together to seal. Using a pair of scissors, trim off only the top edge, not too deep or you will break the seal.

10 Using your thumb and forefinger, crimp the pastry edge. Now make a steam hole in the middle and insert the tip of a 5mm piping nozzle (this will prevent the hole closing).

11 Brush the top of the pie with beaten egg to glaze. Bake for 15 minutes, then lower the oven setting to 170°C/gas mark 3 and bake the pie for a further 30 minutes. Remove from the oven and take off the paper collar. If the pie suddenly begins to slump and lose shape, tie the paper round the pie again and continue to cook for a further 15 minutes. If the pie holds its shape, brush the sides and the top again with beaten egg and return to the oven for a further 30 minutes, or until cooked.

12 To check that the pie is cooked, insert a skewer into the middle through the steam hole, leave it for 10 seconds, then remove and immediately touch it to your inner wrist; it should be hot. If not, cook the pie for a further 15 minutes.

13 Once the pie is cooked, remove from the oven and leave to cool. Prepare the aspic, adding the sage, and pour into the pie (as described on page 135). Allow to set for 3–4 hours.

7

SUET PASTRY

Suet pastry makes a delicious crust for any filling that is rich
with gravy (or syrup in the case of sweet suet pudding dishes)
as it bakes with an appealing golden crust on the outside,
while absorbing just enough of the sauce within to make
it moist and tender. Try baking your favourite stew into a suet
pudding using the methods described in this chapter.
The raising agent in the flour helps to give the pastry a lighter
texture. Unlike most other pastries, suet pastry should not
be rested before use because the raising agent starts working
as soon as the liquid is added.

TECHNIQUE
SUET PASTRY

MAKES enough for a pudding to serve 6–8

350g self-raising flour, plus extra to dust
Large pinch of salt

175g shredded beef or vegetarian suet
100–150ml very cold water

1 Sift the flour and salt into a large bowl. Stir in the suet and rub it into the flour a little with your fingertips, to help break it down.

2 Add 100ml very cold water and, using a cutlery knife, mix everything together. Once you have large flakes, feel them to see if you need more liquid, drawing them to the side and adding more water to the dry flour as necessary.

3 Use your hand to bring the pastry together, feeling the large flakes to ensure there is enough water in the pastry to bring it together comfortably. It should be soft, but not sticky or tacky. Work it in your hands until smooth.

Lining the pudding basin with suet pastry

1 Divide the pastry into 2 unequal pieces, two thirds and one third. On a floured surface, pat out the larger piece into a circle about 2cm thick and 15cm in diameter. Flour one half of the pastry circle (to stop it sticking together) and fold the pastry over to form a half-moon shape.

2 Place the pastry fold side towards you and ridge it lightly with the side of your hand so that the straight side becomes curved and the whole rounded again. You will need to use your hands to encourage the open sides away from you.

3 Open the pastry out like a purse, roughly the shape of the pudding basin. Use it to line the basin (as shown), easing the pastry where necessary to fit, and trimming off the top to leave a 1cm ridge that sits proud of the top.

Covering the pudding basin ready for steaming

1 Cut out one sheet of foil and 2 sheets of greaseproof paper, at least twice the diameter of the top of the pudding basin. Make a small pleat, about 3cm wide, in the middle of the foil. Put one sheet of greaseproof paper on top of the other and make a similar pleat. Lightly butter one side of the double greaseproof paper. Cut a piece of string, the length of your open arms.

2 When the pudding basin is filled and the pudding is ready for steaming, place the greaseproof paper buttered side down on top of the pudding basin. Cover with the sheet of foil and push it down and around the top rim of the pudding basin.

3 Fold the string in half and place the doubled string around the pudding basin under the lip, over the foil. Feed the cut ends between the folded end and tighten the string. Separate the 2 cut ends and bring each string around the pudding basin, still under the lip, then tie tightly in a knot. Put the 2 strings together, take them over the pudding basin to the other side and tuck through the string on the other side, leaving the ends loose to create a handle. Tie the string securely.

4 Lift up the foil around the string to expose the greaseproof paper and trim the paper fairly close to the string. Trim the foil to leave a 3–4cm border. Tuck the foil around the greaseproof paper towards the lip of the pudding basin, ensuring all the greaseproof paper is enclosed in the foil. Your pudding is now ready for steaming.

STEAK AND KIDNEY PUDDING

SERVES 4–6

½ small onion
Handful of flat-leaf parsley
400g beef chuck steak
150g ox kidney
2–3 tbsp plain flour, plus
    extra to dust

Butter, to grease
1 quantity suet pastry
    (see page 140)
Salt and freshly ground black
    pepper

. . . .

You will need a 1 litre pudding basin.

1 Prepare the greaseproof paper, foil and string for steaming, following the instructions on page 140.

2 Peel and very finely dice the onion; you need 2 tsp. Finely chop enough parsley leaves to give 2 tsp. Put both in a large bowl.

3 Trim the beef of excess surface fat and sinew and cut into cubes about 2.5cm square. Prepare the ox kidney by removing the large lobes from the central fat and tubes. Unless the lobes are very large, leave them whole.

4 Put the beef and kidney into a large sieve. Sprinkle over the 2 tbsp flour and shake until the meat is lightly coated. Add the meat to the onion and parsley. Mix together and season well with salt and pepper.

5 Generously butter the pudding basin. Divide the pastry into 2 unequal pieces, two thirds and one third. On a floured surface, pat out the larger piece into a circle about 2cm thick and 15cm in diameter, using a rolling pin or your hands, then use to line the pudding basin (see page 140).

6 Fill with the meat mixture, without packing it too tightly, to leave room for water. Add water to come just below the top pieces of meat.

7 Roll the remaining piece of pastry to a circle 5mm thick, big enough to just cover the filling. Place it on top, wet the edges and press them together so that the lid is sealed to the inside of the pastry lining the pudding basin, not around the outside.

8 Cover with the greaseproof paper and foil and make a string handle (see page 140). Stand the basin on a trivet in a saucepan of boiling water to come halfway up the sides of

the basin and cover with a tight-fitting lid. Alternatively, use a steamer. Steam the pudding for 5–6 hours, topping up the boiling water as necessary so it does not boil dry. It is important to keep the water at a steady boil for the first 30–45 minutes, to ensure the suet in the pastry starts to melt and set with the flour and to achieve a good golden colour.

9 After steaming, carefully lift the pudding basin from the pan, using the string handle, and remove the string, paper and foil. Run a knife around the rim of the basin to release the pudding, invert a plate over the pudding and turn it the right way up so the basin is upside down. Using oven gloves, carefully lift off the pudding basin. Serve at once, with seasonal vegetables.

. . . .

Variations

✳ **Steak and mushroom pudding** Replace the kidneys with 6–8 small chestnut mushrooms, halved or quartered.

✳ **Steak, kidney and oyster pudding** Add a small tin of smoked oysters to the filling – a lovely traditional addition.

. . . .

A note on part-steaming...

✳ You can steam the pudding for at least 3 hours one day, then remove it from the steamer, allow to cool and chill overnight. The pudding can be finished in the steamer the next day. When heating the following day, just ensure that the first 30 minutes – 1 hour is at a generous boil, to get the filling hot as quickly as possible.

PIG CHEEK AND MUSTARD SUET PUDDING

1 leek
1 garlic clove
Handful of flat-leaf parsley
6 sage leaves
550g pig cheeks
About 3 tbsp olive oil
2 tbsp plain flour, plus
    extra to dust

100ml cider
200ml chicken stock
1 tsp wholegrain mustard
Butter, to grease
1 quantity suet pastry
    (see page 140)
Salt and freshly ground
    black pepper

You will need a 1 litre pudding basin.

1 Prepare the greaseproof paper, foil and string for steaming following the instructions on page 140.

2 Thinly slice the leek and wash in cold water to remove any grit, then drain well. Peel and crush the garlic. Finely chop enough parsley leaves to give 1 tbsp. Finely chop the sage.

3 Trim the pig cheeks of any surface fat and sinew, and cut into chunks, about 2.5–3cm. Heat 1 tbsp of the oil in a frying pan over a medium to high heat. Season the meat with salt and, working in batches, brown evenly all over. Pour off any fat from the pan, deglaze the pan with water after each batch and start each new batch with clean oil. Reserve the juices (déglaçage), and as each batch browns transfer the meat to a large bowl. The déglacage can be used in place of some or all of the stock, as long as it does not taste bitter. If it does, discard it.

4 Heat 1 tbsp oil in a saucepan over a medium heat and quickly colour the leeks, stirring, until an even golden brown. Add the garlic and cook for 1 minute, then transfer to a large bowl.

5 Sprinkle the flour over the meat and shake until lightly coated, then add to the leeks and garlic. Add the parsley and sage, mix together and season well with salt and pepper.

6 Put the cider a small saucepan and simmer until reduced by one third. Add the stock, stir in the mustard and allow to cool.

7 Generously butter the pudding basin. Divide the pastry into 2 unequal pieces, two thirds and one third. On a floured surface, pat the larger piece into a circle about 2cm thick and

15cm in diameter, using a rolling pin or your hands, then use to line the pudding basin (see page 140).

8 Fill the pastry lined pudding basin with the meat mixture, without packing it too tightly, to allow room for the stock and cider. Add the liquid to come just below the top pieces of meat.

9 Roll the remaining piece of pastry to a circle 5mm thick, big enough to just cover the pudding filling. Place on top, wet the edges and press together securely so that the lid is sealed to the inside of the pastry lining the pudding basin, not around the outside.

10 Cover with the greaseproof paper and foil, and make a string handle (see page 140).

11 Stand the basin on a trivet in a saucepan of boiling water to come halfway up the sides of the basin and cover with a tight-fitting lid. Alternatively, use a steamer. Steam for 4 hours, topping up the boiling water as necessary so it doesn't boil dry. It is important to keep the water at a generous boil for the first 35–45 minutes, to ensure the suet in the pastry starts to melt and set with the flour and to achieve a good golden colour.

12 After steaming, carefully remove the pudding basin from the saucepan, using the string handle, and remove the string, paper and foil. Run a knife around the top rim of the basin to release the pudding, invert a plate over the pudding and turn it the right way up so the pudding basin is upside down. Using oven gloves, carefully lift off the pudding basin. Serve immediately, with seasonal vegetables.

8

OTHER PASTRIES

There are pastries created using ingredients that are
not found in the classic pastries described so far in this book,
such as polenta to add extra texture. While they may not be
part of the traditional cooking repertoire, the same guiding
principles apply: not overworking the gluten in the flour,
keeping the fat in the mixture cool and avoiding adding too
much liquid to the dough.

EMPANADAS
WITH MOLE DUCK FILLING

MAKES 10

FOR THE FILLING
300g tomatoes
1 onion
4 garlic cloves
2 tbsp vegetable oil
50g pecan nuts
50g pitted dates
120ml fresh orange juice
480ml chicken stock
½–1 dried ancho chilli
½–1 dried habanero chilli
30g good quality dark
   chocolate, 70–80%
   cocoa solids
4 medium duck legs
Salt and freshly ground
   black pepper

FOR THE PASTRY
300g plain flour, plus extra
   to dust
1 tsp salt
60g unsalted butter
60g lard
2 egg yolks, plus 1 beaten
   egg to glaze
100ml chilled water
1 tbsp white wine vinegar

**FOR THE SOURED
CREAM DIP**
300ml soured cream
1–2 tbsp chipotle chilli sauce
   or adobo paste

These Latin American style pasties may take a little time to prepare, but are well worth the effort. The duck is slow cooked until it literally falls off the bone, giving the filling its rich flavour and tender texture. You could always make a double batch of filling which would take very little extra time and freeze some to make another batch of empanadas at a later date.

1 To make the mole sauce, heat the grill to its highest setting. Line a baking tray with foil. Cut the tomatoes into quarters, peel and cut the onion into 6 wedges, and peel the garlic.

2 Put the tomato quarters, garlic and onion wedges on the baking tray and roast under the grill until charred, turning them as necessary until well browned on all sides. Set aside to cool. Heat the oven to 150°C/gas mark 2.

3 Heat the oil in a large frying pan, then add the pecans and stir until lightly toasted, about 3 minutes. Transfer to a plate with a slotted spoon. Add the dates to the pan and fry for about 1 minute, until softened. Remove to the plate with the pecans and set aside.

4 Working in batches if necessary, put the charred tomatoes, garlic and onion, the pecans, dates, orange juice, chicken stock and both chillies in a blender and blend until smooth.

5 Transfer the sauce back to the frying pan and heat gently. Break the chocolate into pieces and stir into the sauce.

6 Place the duck legs in a lidded casserole and season with salt and pepper. Pour over the mole sauce, cover with the lid and cook in the oven for 2 hours. When the duck is cooked, the meat will be very tender and pull away easily from the bone.

7 Meanwhile, to make the pastry, sift the flour and salt into a medium bowl. Cut the butter and lard into small pieces and add to the flour. Cut the fat into the flour, using 2 cutlery knives in a scissor action, then use your fingertips to gently rub it into the flour until the mixture resembles breadcrumbs (see steps 2–4, page 12).

8 Mix the egg yolks, water and vinegar together in a small bowl with a fork until evenly combined. Start by adding half the liquid to the crumb and, using a cutlery knife, distribute the

liquid as quickly as possible (this will create flakes of pastry). Add more liquid to any dry areas of crumb until the flakes come together easily.

9 Pull the pastry together with your hands, shaping it into a log about 8cm in diameter. Wrap in cling film and chill for at least 30 minutes.

10 Transfer the cooked duck legs to a board to cool, then remove and discard the skin. Remove the meat from the bones, then shred it using 2 forks. Put the shredded meat into a bowl.

11 Drain off the fat from the cooked mole sauce and add 6 tbsp of the sauce to the shredded duck; you should have a sticky but not wet mixture. Taste and season with salt and pepper if necessary. Set aside until ready to fill the empanadas.

12 Cut the chilled pastry log into 10 equal rounds. Working with one disc at a time, roll the pastry out on a lightly floured surface to a 12cm diameter circle, using a cutter or a small plate as a guide.

13 Spoon 2–3 tbsp of the duck filling in a line along the middle of the pastry circle, making sure you leave a 2cm clear border around the edge. Brush a little beaten egg around the edge of the pastry (as shown), then fold one side of the empanada over the top of the filling to meet the other edge of the pastry. Press the edges firmly together until you have a 1cm flat seal around the edge of the empanada. Decorate the edges using

the prongs of a fork, pushing firmly around the seal to make the traditional striped pattern. Repeat until you have filled all the empanadas.

14 Chill the empanadas in the fridge for 20–30 minutes. Meanwhile, heat the oven to 200°C/gas mark 6.

15 Just before cooking, brush the surface of the pastry with beaten egg and bake for 25–30 minutes until the pastry is golden brown and the filling is piping hot.

16 While the empanadas are cooking, mix together the soured cream and chipotle sauce and spoon into a bowl to serve with the empanadas.

BUTTERNUT AND PARMESAN POLENTA TART

SERVES 4–6

FOR THE FILLING
1 small or ½ large butternut
    squash (about 1kg)
1 tbsp olive oil
100g Parmesan cheese
Good handful (about 15)
    of sage leaves
2 eggs, plus 2 extra yolks
125ml double cream
Salt and freshly ground
    black pepper

**FOR THE POLENTA AND
CREAM CHEESE PASTRY**
90g cold unsalted butter,
    cut into cubes
90g cream cheese
160g plain flour, plus
    extra to dust
65g fine polenta
1 egg yolk

**This pastry has a delicious crumbly texture, rather like
a savoury version of shortbread. When used to make
tarts, it must be chilled thoroughly until very firm
before blind baking. Try adding chopped herbs or a
little chilli or smoked paprika to vary the flavour. This
recipe can be adapted to make tarts of any size (which
do not need to be baked blind). It will make about
24 individual tarts to serve as a starter, or 36 smaller
canapé-sized tarts to serve with drinks. For one large
tart you will need a 22cm flan tin (or ring).**

1 Heat the oven to 180°C/gas mark 4.

2 For the filling, halve the squash lengthways, if using a small
one, and place cut side up on a baking tray. Drizzle over the
olive oil, season well with salt and pepper and bake for about
45 minutes, or until a cutlery knife slides easily into the flesh.

3 Meanwhile, to make the pastry, put the butter, cream cheese,
flour and polenta in a food processor and pulse to coarse
crumbs. Continue to pulse until the crumbs become lumps.
Add the egg yolk and pulse a couple more times to distribute
it through the dough.

4 Transfer the dough to the work surface and gently bring it
together with your hands (without kneading). Press into a flat
disc, wrap well in cling film and rest in the fridge for 30 minutes
before rolling out.

5 When the squash is cooked, allow it to cool a little, then use
a spoon to scoop out the flesh and mash until smooth with a
potato masher or ricer. Set aside to cool completely.

6 Roll out the pastry on a lightly floured surface to about a
3mm thickness and use to line the 22cm flan tin (see page 18).
Cover with cling film and chill in the fridge until firm to the
touch, 20–30 minutes.

7 Blind bake the pastry for 12 minutes (see page 20), ensuring
the paper is pushed well into the corners of the pastry and
the excess paper is folded over the edge of the pastry case, to
help prevent the pastry from browning. Remove the beans and
paper, taking care as the pastry will still be very soft. Bake for a
further 3–4 minutes until the pastry is pale golden brown with
no grey patches.

8 Remove from the oven and leave to cool slightly. Reduce the
oven temperature to 150°C/gas mark 2.

9 To make the filling, grate the Parmesan and chop the sage
leaves. Lightly beat together the whole eggs, yolks, cream,
Parmesan and the puréed butternut squash. Add the chopped
sage and salt and pepper to taste.

10 Spoon or pour the filling into the pastry case, filling the case
almost to the top. Bake for 30–40 minutes until just set. Serve
warm or at room temperature.

PEAR AND MULLED WINE POLENTA TART

SERVES 6–8

FOR THE SWEET POLENTA PASTRY	FOR THE PEARS
170g plain flour	750ml red wine
50g fine polenta, plus 1 tbsp	100–150g caster sugar
Pinch of salt	10 cloves
100g butter, softened	5 strips of thinly pared lemon zest
100g caster sugar	2 cinnamon sticks
2 egg yolks	12 pears, ideally Conference

This tart brings together the intense colour of wine-poached fruit and warm flavours of Christmas mulling spices in a lovely, almost-shortbready polenta pastry. You will need a 24cm flan tin (or ring).

1 To make the pastry, sift the flour, 50g polenta and salt onto a work surface and, using the side of your hand, spread it into a large ring. Place the softened butter, in one piece, in the middle and, using the fingertips of one hand, push down ('peck') on the butter to soften it a little more, but without it becoming greasy; it should be uniformly soft, but still cold (see page 42).

2 Sprinkle over the sugar and continue to 'peck' until the sugar is just fully incorporated. Add the egg yolk to the butter and sugar mixture and continue to 'peck' until the egg yolk is fully incorporated and there is no streakiness in the pastry.

3 Using a palette knife, flick all the flour mix onto the butter, sugar and egg yolks and, using the edge of the knife, 'chop' the flour into the butter and sugar mixture. This technique helps to keep the flour from being overworked. Use the palette knife to lift any flour left on the work surface to the top occasionally. As you continue to do this, you will create large flakes of pastry. Continue until there are no obvious dry floury bits among the pastry; it should be a fairly uniform even colour.

4 Shape the pastry into a long sausage and, using the palette knife on its side, scrape a little of the large flakes together at a time. This will finally bring the pastry together and is called 'fraisering' (see page 42). As more pastry sticks to the palette knife, scrape it off using a cutlery knife to avoid overworking it. Continue until all the pastry is fraisered.

5 Bring the pastry together with your hands, divide in two and shape each half into a flat disc. Wrap well in cling film and chill.

6 For the filling, put the wine, sugar, cloves, lemon zest and cinnamon sticks in a medium saucepan and simmer over a medium heat until reduced by about one fifth. Meanwhile, peel the pears, cut them in half lengthways and remove the core. Cut lengthways into 5mm slices, add them to the wine and cook at the barest simmer for 15–20 minutes (or less if very ripe) until tender. Drain carefully and allow to cool. Strain the wine into a saucepan and discard the flavourings. Simmer until reduced to a syrupy consistency, then set aside for serving.

7 Roll out one of the pastry discs on a floured surface to a 5mm thickness and use to line a 24cm flan tin (see page 18). Chill until firm. Heat the oven to 200°C/gas mark 6.

8 Blind bake the pastry (see page 20) for 15–20 minutes, then remove the paper and beans and bake for a further 5 minutes, or until the pastry looks dry and feels sandy to the touch.

9 Sprinkle the 1 tbsp polenta over the pastry and layer the pears into the pastry case, packing them in quite firmly. Roll out the remaining pastry disc to 5mm thick and, using a 5–6cm pastry cutter, stamp out as many circles as necessary to cover the pears. Start from the edge of the pastry at the rim, slightly overlapping the circles as you lay them on top of the pears.

10 Bake for about 30 minutes, covering with greaseproof paper after 20 minutes if it shows signs of becoming too brown. The pastry should be a golden colour with no grey patches. Remove from the oven and allow to cool a little before removing from the tin. Serve warm with the reduced syrup and crème fraîche.

TARTE TATIN

MAKES 6–8

FOR THE PASTRY
170g plain flour, plus extra
    to dust
55g ground rice
Pinch of salt
140g butter
50g caster sugar
1 egg

FOR THE FILLING
1.5kg dessert apples
1 lemon
100g butter
100g granulated sugar

This version of a classic tarte tatin adds ground rice to a basic shortcrust pastry, which produces a delicious texture, although puff pastry is more traditional for a tatin. You will need a tatin mould or a heavy-based ovenproof frying pan, about 24cm in diameter, that will fit in your oven.

1 To make the pastry, sift the flour, ground rice and salt into a large bowl. Cut the butter into small pieces and add to the bowl. Using 2 cutlery knives and working in a scissor action, cut the butter into the flour, then rub it in with your fingertips until the mixture resembles fine breadcrumbs (see steps 2–4, page 12). Stir in the sugar. Beat the egg with a fork, then using a cutlery knife, add enough to bind the dough together.

2 Shape the pastry into a flat disc, place between 2 sheets of baking parchment and roll gently to a circle the size of your ovenproof frying pan, no thinner than 5mm. Chill in the fridge until firm.

3 For the filling, peel, quarter and core the apples and finely grate the lemon zest. Heat the oven to 190°C/gas mark 5.

4 Melt the butter in the frying pan over a low heat. Add the sugar and cook gently until the sugar has started to melt and turn a toffee colour.

5 Arrange the first layer of apple quarters, rounded side down, on top of the melted butter and sugar. Sprinkle over the lemon zest and continue to layer on the apples, arranging the next layer rounded side up and fitting neatly in the spaces in the bottom layer.

6 Continue to cook over a low to medium heat. Initially the apples will release juice and prevent the butter and sugar from caramelising, but as the juice mixes with the butter and sugar it will become a homogeneous sauce. Then as the juice evaporates, the butter and sugar will begin to caramelise again.

7 Continue cooking until the caramel is deep golden, and the apples have taken on the same colour, about 15–20 minutes; you will be able to smell the caramelisation. You may need to move the frying pan around over the heat to ensure even caramelisation. Carefully lift up the apples from time to time, using a palette knife, to check the underside (as shown). Remove the frying pan from the heat and place on a lipped baking tray.

8 Take the pastry out of the fridge and peel away one layer of parchment. Lay the pastry on top of the apples and peel off the other layer of parchment. Press down lightly, particularly over the edge of the frying pan (as shown) so that the heat of the frying pan cuts through the pastry. Remove any excess pastry. Transfer to the oven and bake for 25–30 minutes until the pastry is golden.

9 Remove from the oven and allow to cool slightly for a few minutes. Now carefully invert a plate over the frying pan (as shown) and turn both the frying pan and plate over, so the frying pan is uppermost. Ideally, cover your forearms with a cloth as you do this to protect them from any hot caramel that may be released. Lower the plate and frying pan to the work surface and carefully lift off the frying pan to reveal the golden apples and caramel sauce. Best served warm, with ice cream, pouring cream or crème fraîche.

CRÈME PÂTISSIÈRE

MAKES 300ml	
300ml whole milk	50g caster sugar
½ vanilla pod or a few drops of vanilla extract	15g plain flour
3 egg yolks	15g cornflour

Crème pâtissière, or pastry cream, is used as a sweet filling, in éclairs and millefeuille, for example. It can be lightened by folding in 100ml lightly whipped double cream at the end.

1 Put the milk in a saucepan. Split the vanilla pod, if using, down one side, then scrape out the seeds. Add the pod and seeds to the milk and place the pan over a medium heat. Heat gently until steaming. Just before it bubbles, take off the heat and remove the vanilla pod and any skin that has formed.

2 Mix the egg yolks and sugar together in a bowl. Add a splash of the hot milk, then the flours. Mix well, ensuring there are no lumps. Gradually stir in the remaining milk. Return the mixture to a clean pan and place over a low to medium heat. Bring to the boil, stirring. It will go lumpy, but stir vigorously and it will become smooth. Turn the heat down and simmer for 2 minutes.

3 Remove from the heat and add the vanilla extract, if using. Transfer to a bowl and lay a disc of greaseproof paper on the surface, to prevent a skin forming. Set aside to cool.

4 Once cool, transfer the crème pâtissière to a food processor and blend until soft and smooth. It is now ready for use.

Variations

✱ **Almond crème pâtissière** Stir 2 tbsp ground almonds and ½–1 tsp Amaretto, to taste, into the finished mixture.

✱ **Coffee crème pâtissière** Replace 30–50ml of the milk with strong espresso coffee, to taste.

SUGAR SYRUP

MAKES about 500ml	
250g granulated sugar	500ml water

This is a basic syrup that can be made in a large quantity and kept in the fridge for general purpose use, such as making coulis or macerating fruit.

1 Put the sugar and water in a medium saucepan. Place over a low heat to dissolve the sugar, using the handle of a wooden spoon to gently agitate it and prevent it from 'caking' on the bottom of the pan. Avoid splashing syrup up the sides.

2 Once the sugar has dissolved, use a pastry brush dipped in water to brush down the sides of the pan, to wash any remaining sugar crystals down into the syrup.

3 Turn the heat up and do not stir from this point. Bring the syrup to the boil and boil steadily for 5 minutes. Take off the heat, cool and keep covered until needed.

APRICOT GLAZE

MAKES enough to glaze a 24cm tart	
250g apricot jam (not whole fruit)	2–3 tbsp water (optional) 1 lemon

1 Put the jam into a small saucepan. Using a swivel peeler, pare a strip or two of lemon zest, add to the pan and heat gently, without stirring, until the jam has melted, without letting it boil. If the jam is very thick add 2–3 tbsp warm water to loosen it, then pass through a fine sieve into a bowl, discarding the zest.

2 Adjust the consistency with a little more warm water until the glaze coats a pastry brush evenly and is the consistency of runny honey. It should come off the brush in a single stream for 2–3cm, then start to drip off. Some jam will not need any water added, some will need more, but take care as too much water will thin the jam too much and it will not adhere properly.

3 When applying glaze, dab it on the fruit. As you use the glaze, keep checking the consistency and adding water as necessary, as it will thicken as it cools.

Variation

✱ **Redcurrant glaze** Replace the apricot jam with redcurrant jelly. Generally, on warming, redcurrant jelly melts to a much looser consistency, so you won't need to add as much water.

RASPBERRY COULIS

MAKES 250ml	
50g granulated sugar 75ml water 250g raspberries (fresh or defrosted frozen ones)	Squeeze of lemon juice (optional)

1 Put the sugar and water into a saucepan. Place over a low heat to dissolve the sugar, using the handle of a wooden spoon to gently agitate the sugar to stop it 'caking' on the bottom of the pan. Try to avoid splashing syrup up the sides of the pan.

2 Once the sugar is dissolved, use a pastry brush dipped in water to brush down the sides of the pan, to wash any remaining sugar crystals down into the syrup.

3 Turn the heat up, stop stirring from this point, and bring the syrup to the boil for 2 minutes, then remove from the heat and allow to cool slightly.

4 Put the berries in a food processor with half the sugar syrup and blend to a purée. Strain through a fine sieve into a bowl. Taste and adjust the consistency and sweetness with lemon juice or sugar syrup. It should have a 'floodable' consistency.

Variations

✱ Use other soft fruit, such as strawberries or blueberries in place of the raspberries. Fruit juice can be used to thin the coulis.

EQUIPMENT

Equipment

Trays and tins for baking do not need to be non-stick, but should be solid enough not to warp when they are heated.

Scales A set of good scales is imperative – electronic scales are more accurate when measuring smaller quantities

Chopping boards Use separate boards for raw and cooked foods

Bowls A selection of various sizes, glass or stainless steel

Measuring jug

Juicer

Baking sheets Some flat and some with a lip

Shallow baking tray

Roasting tin

Wire cooling rack

Loose-based flan tins 22 and 24cm

Loose-based individual flan tins 10cm, 12cm

Flan rings 24cm

12-hole shallow bun trays Useful to have 2 of these

Muffin tins

Mini-muffin tins

Pie dishes A selection of sizes, including 1 litre and 1.2 litre dishes

Casseroles with lids A selection of sizes

Oven gloves

Utensils

Good kitchen tools make work in the kitchen easier and more efficient. The following are particularly useful when baking pastries:

Measuring spoons

Wooden spoons

Rolling pin

Kitchen scissors (a sturdy pair)

Swivel vegetable peeler

Apple corer

Pastry cutters

Palette knife

Spatula (heat-resistant)

Fine grater

Zester

Pans

Saucepans At least three in a range of sizes from 18–28cm

Frying pans At least two in different sizes from 16–28cm

Knives

Large cook's knife Important for fine slicing, fine chopping and many other food preparation tasks

Paring knife For controlled cutting of small ingredients

Pastry knife A long serrated knife is used for cutting pastries (also cakes and breads) without crumbling or tearing

Small serrated knife This is very useful for preparing fruit

Small electrical equipment

Electric mixer A free-standing mixer is probably the most controllable machine for making consistently good pastry

Food processor Useful for making pastry, but care is needed to avoid over-processing

Blender A free-standing blender for purées and coulis

Hand-held stick blender Also useful for purées and coulis

Paper/lining products

Greaseproof paper

Baking parchment/silicone paper

Aluminium foil

Cling film

Non-stick baking mats (re-usable)

GLOSSARY

BLANCH To part-cook vegetables quickly in boiling water, usually before refreshing in cold water, to stop the cooking and set the colour. It is also used to loosen the skins of tomatoes, or mellow flavour and/or reduce the salt.

BLIND BAKE To line a pastry case with a circle of greaseproof paper (a cartouche), fill it with baking beans and bake before the filling is added. The layer of beans helps the pastry case to hold its shape as it cooks. The beans are then removed with the paper and the pastry case is returned to the oven to dry the base (or cook the pastry fully if the filling won't be cooked in the case.)

BOIL To cook food submerged in liquid heated so that the bubbles are constant and vigorous.

BROWN To fry or roast to achieve colour and flavour as the natural sugars caramelise, such as pieces of beef for a stew.

CARAMEL Sugar turned to a deep terracotta brown by heating.

CARAMELISE See Brown (above).

CARTOUCHE A circle of greaseproof paper used dry during blind baking, or wet pressed onto sweating onions or other vegetables under a lid, to allow the food to soften without browning.

CHILL To cool food down in the fridge or using an ice bath, ideally to 4°C.

COULIS A thin purée, usually of fruit with a little sugar syrup.

CREAM To beat together ingredients to incorporate air, typically butter and sugar.

CUT UP (OR KNOCK UP) To cut into the edge of raw layered pastry, holding the knife blade horizontally, to encourage it to rise, and the layers to be more defined during cooking.

DEGLAZE To add liquid, usually wine or water, to a pan after frying and stirring/scraping to loosen the sediment on the bottom so it can be incorporated into the sauce to add flavour.

DÉTREMPE The base dough of a layered pastry.

DROPPING CONSISTENCY When a mixture will drop reluctantly from a spoon if it is tapped on the side of the bowl or pan, neither pouring off nor continuing to stick to the spoon.

EGG WASH Beaten egg, sometimes salted, brushed onto pastry to give it colour and shine.

ENRICH To add cream, butter or a cream and egg yolk mixture to a sauce or other dish to thicken and enhance the flavour.

FOLD To combine two or more mixtures using a large metal spoon or spatula and a lifting and turning motion to avoid destroying the air bubbles. Usually one of the mixtures is more airy and delicate than the other.

FRAISER When making an enriched pastry, to use a palette knife to 'scrape' and combine the ingredients.

GLAZE To lend a glossy finish. A glaze may be applied before or after cooking. For example, an egg glaze is applied to pastry prior to baking, while an apricot glaze is brushed over the warm fruit in a tart on removing from the oven.

INFUSE To immerse aromatic ingredients, such as herbs or spices, in a hot liquid to flavour it.

JULIENNE Vegetables, fresh ginger or citrus zest cut into thin, matchstick-sized pieces.

LET DOWN To thin an overly thick sauce with a little liquid, normally stock or water in savoury dishes, to achieve the desired consistency.

LIGHTEN To incorporate air into a dish, by carefully folding in egg whites or lightly whipped cream for example.

MACERATE To soak food, usually fruit, in a flavoured liquid, to soften it and facilitate the exchange of flavours, for example orange segments in a cinnamon-flavoured syrup.

NEEDLESHREDS Finely and evenly cut shreds of citrus zest, typically used as a garnish.

PANADE The thick base mixture of a soufflé or choux pastry. Made from butter, flour and milk or water, it is also used as a binding mixture.

PINCH An approximate quantity that can be pinched between the thumb and forefinger, less than ⅛ tsp.

PITH The soft white layer directly beneath the coloured zest of citrus fruit. It is invariably bitter in flavour and avoided when zesting the fruit.

POACH To submerge food in liquid that is hot yet barely trembling (never bubbling), on the hob or in the oven. Ideal for cooking delicate food.

PURÉE Usually vegetables or fruit, blended and/ or sieved until smooth.

REDUCE To rapidly boil a liquid, such as a stock or sauce, to concentrate the flavour by evaporating some of the liquid.

REFRESH To plunge blanched or boiled vegetables into cold water to stop the cooking and set the colour, before draining.

RELAX OR REST To set pastry aside in a cool place, usually the fridge, to allow the gluten to relax before baking. This helps to minimise shrinking in the oven.

ROUX Equal quantities of butter and flour, cooked together and used to thicken a measured quantity of liquid, such as for a white sauce.

RUB IN To rub small pieces of butter into flour with the fingertips until the mixture resembles breadcrumbs.

SAUTÉ To brown small pieces of food in butter or oil over a high heat, shaking the pan or stirring to ensure the ingredients colour quickly and evenly.

SCALD To heat a liquid (milk, usually) until on the verge of boiling. At scalding point, steam is escaping and bubbles are starting to form around the edge of the pan.

SCORE To make shallow or deep cuts in the surface of pastry or other food with a sharp knife.

SEASON Usually simply to flavour with salt and pepper, but it can also involve adjusting acidity with lemon juice or sweetness by adding sugar. The term also describes rubbing a pan with oil and salt to make it non-stick.

SIMMER To cook food submerged in liquid, heated to a level that ensures small bubbles constantly appear around the edge of the pan.

STEAM To cook food in hot vapour, usually from boiling water. The food sits in a perforated (or permeable) container and cooks in the steam that surrounds it. In indirect steaming, the food is protected from the steam itself but cooks in the heat created by it; a suet pudding is an example.

WELL A hollow in a mound of flour in a bowl or on the work surface, created to contain the liquid ingredients before they are incorporated.

ZEST The coloured outer skin of citrus fruit used for flavouring, which must be carefully removed from the bitter white pith before it is added. 'To zest' describes the action of finely paring the zest from citrus fruit, using a zester.

INDEX

ACKNOWLEDGEMENTS

The recipes in this book have been compiled, adapted and edited by Jenny Stringer, Claire Macdonald and Camilla Schneideman, but the authors are a large collection of Leiths staff and visiting teachers, past and present. Thank you to everyone who wrote recipes for this book, notably: Louisa Bradford, Max Clark, Rupert Holden, Claire Macdonald, Heli Miles, Shenley Moore, Mel Ryder, Camilla Schneideman, Jenny Stringer, Ron Sweetser and Tom Thexton.

But with the sheer number of talented cooks around us at the school, we must say a big thank you to everyone who has helped develop ideas for this book, tested the recipes and given valuable feedback during the tasting sessions. Special thanks must go to Helene Robinson-Moltke, Ansobe Smal and Belinda Spinney who were at the photo shoots.

Thank you to the team at Quadrille. We have been extremely lucky to continue our relationship with our editor Janet Illsley. Janet's patience with the authors is legendary – deadlines with this number of people involved required military organisation and, as ever, we are incredibly grateful for her wisdom. Thank you too Sally Somers for editing the copy.

Thank you to the team that worked together on the design and photography for this book: Peter Cassidy for his brilliant photography, Gabriella Le Grazie for her art direction, Emily Kydd and Emily Quah (both Leiths graduates) for the food styling. We are thrilled with the new style Katherine Keeble has created for this series of books, so thank you all.

CREATIVE DIRECTOR Helen Lewis
PROJECT EDITOR Janet Illsley
DESIGN Katherine Keeble
ART DIRECTION Gabriella Le Grazie
PHOTOGRAPHER Peter Cassidy
FOOD STYLISTS Emily Kydd and Emily Quah
LEITHS CONSULTANTS Helene Robinson-Moltke, Ansobe Smal and Belinda Spinney
COPY EDITOR Sally Somers
PROPS STYLISTS Iris Bromet and Cynthia Inions
PRODUCTION Vincent Smith, Tom Moore

First published in 2015 by
Quadrille Publishing Limited
www.quadrille.co.uk

Text © 2015 Leiths School of Food and Wine
Photography © 2015 Peter Cassidy
Design and layout © 2015 Quadrille Publishing Limited

The rights of the author have been asserted.

Cataloguing in Publication Data: a catalogue record for this book is available from the British Library.

ISBN 978 184949 5516

Printed in China